From the Old Diplomacy
to the New, 1865–1900

The Crowell American History Series

JOHN HOPE FRANKLIN & ABRAHAM S. EISENSTADT, *Editors*

Robert L. Beisner
THE AMERICAN UNIVERSITY

From the Old Diplomacy to the New, 1865–1900

Thomas Y. Crowell Company
NEW YORK
ESTABLISHED 1834

Library of Congress Cataloging in Publication Data

BEISNER, ROBERT L
   From the old diplomacy to the new, 1865–1900.

   (Crowell American history series)
   Includes bibliographical references.
      1. United States—Foreign relations—1865–1898.
I. Title.
E661.7.B44   327.73   74–7001
ISBN 0–690–00626–8

Series design by Judith Woracek Barry

Manufactured in the United States of America

1   2   3   4   5   6   7   8   9   10

For my parents,
E. J. and Charlene Beisner

EDITORS' FOREWORD

It is a commonplace that each age writes its own history, for the reason that man sees the past in the foreshortened perspective of his own experience. This has certainly been true of the writing of American history. The purpose of our historical writing remains constant: to offer us a more certain sense of where we are going by indicating the road we have taken in getting there. But it is precisely because our own generation is redefining its direction, the way other generations have redefined theirs before us, that the substance of our historical writing is changing. We are thinking anew of our direction because of our newer values and premises, our newer sense of how we can best fulfill the goals of our society, our newer outlook on the meaning of American life. Thus, the vitality of the present inspires the vitality of our writing about the past.

It is the plan of the *Crowell American History Series* to offer the reader a survey of the point of arrival of recent scholarship on the central themes and problems of American history. The scholars we have invited to do the respective volumes of the series are younger individuals whose monographs have been well received by their peers and who have demonstrated their mastery of the subjects on which they are writing. The author of each volume has undertaken to present a summation of the principal lines of discussion that historians of a particular subject have been pursuing. However, he has not written a mere digest of historical literature. The author has been concerned, moreover, to offer the reader a sufficient factual and narrative account to help him perceive the larger dimensions of the subject. Each author, moreover, has arrived at his own conclusions about those aspects of his subject that have been matters of difference and controversy. In effect, he has written not only about where the subject stands in historiography but also about where he himself stands on the subject. And each volume concludes with an extensive critical essay on authorities.

The books in this series are designed for use in the basic course in American history, although they could be used, with great benefit, in advanced courses as well. Such a series has a particular utility in times such as these, when the traditional format of our American history courses is being altered to accommodate a greater diversity of texts and reading materials. The series offers a number of distinct advantages. It extends and deepens the dimensions of course work in American history. In proceeding beyond the confines of the traditional textbook, it makes clear that the study of our past is, more than the student might otherwise infer, at once complex, sophisticated, and profound. It presents American history as a subject of continuing vitality and fresh investigation. The work of experts in their respective fields, it opens up to the student the rich findings of historical inquiry. It invites the student to join with his older and more experienced colleagues in pondering anew the major themes and problems of our past. It challenges the student to participate actively in exploring American history and to seek out its wider reaches on his own.

John Hope Franklin
Abraham S. Eisenstadt

ACKNOWLEDGMENTS

Thanks are due to The American University for fellowships in 1970 and 1972 that freed me from summer teaching and advanced progress on this book; to Robert Carola of Thomas Y. Crowell Company for his gracious patience with a rather tardy author; to John Hope Franklin, Abraham S. Eisenstadt, and two helpful anonymous readers for their critical evaluation of the manuscript and suggestions for improvement; to Michael Roskin for initially acquainting me with the paradigm theory discussed in these pages (but who is in no way responsible for my application of it to the 1865–1900 period of American diplomacy); to many of my students, especially Wayne Knight, Richard Norment, and William Sweeney, for offering helpful criticisms of classroom lectures and office-hours monologues in which I tried out early versions of my arguments; to my children, John and Katharine, for relinquishing some of the fun time supposedly available to academic families; and to my talented wife, Mary, for so improving this book by her skillful touch with word, phrase, sentence, paragraph, and idea as to qualify as coauthor. She agrees with me, however, that criticisms of this book should be directed at none of those mentioned above, but at me, the responsible party.

CONTENTS

Introduction

This volume is not intended to provide a comprehensive factual narrative of American foreign relations in the years 1865 to 1900 but rather, in the hope that the reader is already familiar with the details or is concurrently being exposed to them in a textbook, to offer an analysis of the highlights of the period and an evaluation of recent scholarship in the field.

A beginning student is often puzzled by his encounter with conflicting historical interpretations. I hope to resolve some of that puzzlement in the following pages through my discussion of the specific issues—such as the causes of the Spanish-American

War—that have generated contradictory points of view. But some of the most significant and bewildering differences among historians are not of a nature to be treated adequately in a strictly chronological narrative. Thus this book opens with a chapter devoted to a discussion of the fundamental circumstances, traditions, and ideas that shaped the conduct of United States diplomacy throughout the period under consideration and an analysis of several knotty historiographical controversies that affect one's understanding of the entire era.

Since I wish to leave the reader with more than a description of alternative interpretations, I am proposing a new way to look at these years, one that will certainly not supersede all others but will afford, I hope, a way of reconciling some earlier views usually thought to be in conflict. This interpretation first appears in Chapter Two, which is concerned, in the main, with a discussion of American foreign policy in the years from 1865 to 1889. Chapter Three contains an analysis of the fundamental change in policy that occurred in the late 1880s and early 1890s. Chapter Four deals with the early years (1889–97) of this new era, and Chapter Five with its culmination in the administration of William McKinley (1897–1901). These last three chapters, collectively, form an important unit since it is apparent that at some time around the year 1890 the United States entered upon a more aggressive and expansionist phase in its diplomatic history and reached out into the world in an increasingly determined and deliberate fashion. This change did not occur overnight—we cannot suppose that a secretary of state rolled out of bed one morning, rubbed his eyes, and exclaimed, "This morning we are a great power!" Nor was the change total, for history is never so accommodating. But by the mid-nineties at the latest, American policymakers had begun to see foreign affairs from a new perspective, to confront the international world with new assumptions and concerns, and to seek new objectives. One of the prime purposes of this book is to explain the nature of this change and the reasons for its advent.

ONE

Underlying Themes and Issues

CIRCUMSTANTIAL GIVENS

Underlying any nation's foreign policy are certain basic "givens"
—circumstances, conditions, institutions, beliefs, and attitudes
—that guide its diplomacy toward certain goals and away from
others, basic components that define the perimeters of policy
within which both dangers and opportunities are restricted.
Especially important in the period under study were six "givens"
of a circumstantial character: European diplomacy, economic

developments, public opinion, Senate power, politics, and the available instruments of foreign affairs; and four influential traditions: the American Mission, isolationism, the Monroe Doctrine, and the Open Door.

European Diplomacy. On occasion American policymakers have found their job made easier by conflicts among European states. This phenomenon, described by Samuel F. Bemis as "America's Advantage from Europe's Distress," was especially important in the early years of the Republic when the wars of the French Revolution and Napoleon tore Europe apart and created opportunities for certain American diplomatic triumphs that would not otherwise have been possible. But even after relative tranquillity returned to Europe, Americans were able to exploit European tensions in some instances. Prussia's drive for German hegemony, for example, contributed to the withdrawal of French troops from Mexico in 1866-67; Russian denunciation of the Black Sea Treaty and the outbreak of the Franco-Prussian War in 1870 pushed Great Britain toward an amicable settlement of the *Alabama* controversy that had arisen during the Civil War; and during the Anglo-American crisis of 1895-96 over the Venezuelan border with British Guiana, Britain again proved a weaker adversary than expected, this time because of the threat of being diplomatically isolated on the Continent and challenged in South Africa.

Economic Developments. An even more important "given" influencing American foreign policy was the nation's rapid industrialization. The precise extent of this influence on United States officials is the subject of a noisy debate among scholars that will be examined later in the chapter. In any case, it is clear that the emergence of the United States as the world's leading industrial producer added significantly to its potential impact on international relations, reduced southern and rural influence in the formulation of American policy, made diplomats more aware of the importance of promoting U.S. exports, and increased the areas of the world in which Americans felt their national interests were involved.

Public Opinion. A factor of fundamental domestic importance, yet always difficult to evaluate, was public opinion. It certainly played a role in the prolongation of the *Alabama* claims controversy, in pushing the United States and Spain to the brink of war in the 1870s, and in toppling them over the brink in 1898. Public opinion killed President Grant's effort to annex Santo Domingo in 1870. It put brakes on the rapprochement with Great Britain at the end of the century. Dozens of examples come to mind, yet historians have found it nearly impossible to weigh the exact impact of public opinion at any point in time. Then, as now, opinion could be created out of whole cloth or adroitly manipulated by a determined administration. Because of public indifference or ignorance, minor or peripheral policies could often be executed within an opinion vacuum. Those elements of the population interested in foreign affairs shifted in numbers and identity: one segment might give close attention to British issues, another to Chinese issues. And as Ernest R. May points out in *American Imperialism: A Speculative Essay* (1968), tiny elites in a few metropolitan areas of the country dominated the foreign-policy opinions of thousands of followers. The political leader who glanced over his shoulder to see if the "public" supported him might really have been seeking the support, consciously or unconsciously, of a few acknowledged leaders of opinion and influential newspapers. On other occasions his backward glance might have been directed to the leaders of special interest and ethnic groups, whether steel manufacturers, food processors, missionaries, or Irish-Americans.

The Senate. Always present for executive policymakers to contend with was Congress, and especially the Senate, whose members possessed a haughty institutional pride and certain exclusive constitutional prerogatives in declaring war, approving treaties, and confirming diplomatic appointments. In his novel *Democracy*, Henry Adams spoke of a government "of the people, by the people, for the Senate." He had in mind the body of men who, among other things, blocked the annexation of Santo Domingo, scrapped a long series of reciprocal trade agreements, rejected an arbitration agreement with Great Britain (the Olney-Pauncefotc Treaty of 1897), nearly defeated the peace treaty concluding the Spanish-American War, and forced renegotiation of the pact that cleared the way for exclusive American control of an isthmian canal (the first Hay-Pauncefote Treaty, 1900). A far greater number of accords never got past the talking stage or were never submitted for ratification because of known Senate hostility to them.

Politics. Partisan politics, which affected presidents and secretaries of state just as much as congressmen, was another constant. Thus it should come as no great surprise that the outrageous Benjamin F. Butler hoped that Anglo-American talks on the *Alabama* issue would break down and, in so doing, insure a GOP victory in the 1872 elections; or that, conversely, the Grant administration was prompted to settle this issue partly to outflank dissident Liberal Republicans; or that James G. Blaine saw a Pan-American conference in 1881 as a step toward a presidential nomination in 1884, that Republicans defeated an important Canadian fisheries agreement in 1888 because a Democratic administration had negotiated it, or that President Cleveland agreed to the exclusion of Chinese immigrants because the California electorate demanded it. A more responsible treatment of foreign affairs appeared in the nineties, as we shall see, but the impact of partisan politics had by no means disappeared. Foreign affairs, not yet inextricably linked with "national security," could still be employed for domestic political objectives without great risk of rebuke. No one had yet coined the phrase, "bipartisan foreign policy."

Instruments of Foreign Affairs. Those who formulated and conducted American foreign policy had of necessity to operate with the instruments of international power available to them: the diplomatic corps, the army, and the navy. The first is discussed later in this chapter; suffice it to say at this point that during most of the era, with occasional exceptions, the diplomats of the United States were inexperienced, unprofessional, and often astonishingly clumsy. Even less impressive was the diminutive American army, which usually numbered around 28,000 men until the onset of the Spanish-American War. In

1890 the army ranked about thirteenth in the world, smaller than Bulgaria's; and since most of its units were scattered here and there, fighting Indians, exploring mountain passes, or dredging river channels, it ranked even lower as a force to contend with in international affairs. This was tolerable and even appropriate as long as American policymakers had nothing too ambitious in mind, but the outbreak of war in 1898 demanded speedy expansion, and by 1900 nearly 100,000 men wore the national colors. Even then, what with 9,500 soldiers in Cuba and 61,000 more fighting rebels in the Philippines, the United States was hard pressed to find a few thousand men for assignment to the international force that suppressed China's Boxer Rebellion in 1900.

Given America's geographical circumstances and primary diplomatic interests, it was of greater importance in the late nineteenth century to maintain a good navy than a large army. But the vigorous Union navy had been dismantled after the Civil War, and its poor remnant often seemed as inadequate as the army in the years that followed. Any American official setting policy in the Caribbean in the 1870s, for instance, was forced to move cautiously, realizing that many American war vessels in the area were powered by boilers so antiquated they could make only $4\frac{1}{2}$ of the 12 knots they were designed for. Possibly more dangerous to their crews than any enemy, the ships of the United States Navy were described by future Secretary of the Navy John D. Long in 1885 as "an alphabet of floating wash-tubs."

The navy's condition improved during the Arthur administration in the early eighties under the leadership of Secretary of the Navy William E. Chandler and Commodore Stephen B. Luce (see J. A. S. Grenville and G. B. Young, *Politics, Strategy and American Diplomacy: Studies in Foreign Policy, 1873–1917* [1966], and Kenneth J. Hagan, *American Gunboat Diplomacy and the Old Navy, 1877–1889* [1973], for Luce's important role). Under their aegis Captain Alfred T. Mahan's remarkable talents found a platform in the new Naval War College, and a modest rebuilding program was begun. The pace of construction quickened in the 1890s. By 1898 the navy could easily outdo Spain's ramshackle fleets, but the easy victories of 1898 obscured remaining weaknesses from view. Just four years earlier a ship ordered to Nicaragua during the Corinto Affair (Chapter Four) sank ignominiously en route, and on the eve of the 1898 war with Spain the navy possessed only eight heavily armored ships, none of which met the European standard of "battleship."

Despite its shortcomings, the U.S. Navy at times played an important role in American diplomacy during this era. In 1872 Commander Richard W. Meade, acting on his own, arranged exclusive U.S. control of the Samoan harbor of Pago Pago (only to have the Senate reject his handiwork). Captain Robert W. Shufeldt's 1878 voyage along the coast of West Africa aroused American interest in that continent, and four years later the same officer inaugurated United States relations with Korea. In the years 1897–1909, as William R. Braisted has observed, the navy did not "dictate American foreign policy," but "naval considerations were often determining factors in the formulation of the Far Eastern policies of the United States" (*The United States Navy in the Pacific, 1897–1909*, [1958]).

That American government officials, journalists, and the general public complacently tolerated such an unimpressive array of diplomatic instruments and permitted obscure naval officers to take far-reaching diplomatic initiatives suggests how little inclination there was in Gilded Age Washington to pursue a well-defined and centrally controlled "foreign policy." Until the 1890s this vacuum in centralized policymaking was far more the rule than the exception—the sign of a nation still lacking a coherent approach to international affairs.

AMERICAN BELIEFS AND TRADITIONS

"Givens" of a circumstantial nature may have set the general boundaries of American diplomacy, but within those boundaries the specific directions of American foreign policy were determined by beliefs and traditions that required little conscious thought or reflection. They were ingrained—"given" in the strictest sense of the word.

The American Mission. Basic among American beliefs—for diplomatic officials as well as their countrymen—was the conviction that the people of the United States possessed a special world mission. They were destined not merely to inhabit the earth, but to create a free nation and develop a Way of Life (as it would later be called) never before achieved in history. Since this concept made Americans feel inherently superior to all other peoples, it did not matter that their army was numerically inferior to Bulgaria's. What was a large army compared to such a high calling? Woodrow Wilson would eventually define this mission as the positive obligation to spread American principles and institutions to the rest of the world; the post–Civil War generation, however, was content to interpret it in passive terms, holding that America's duty was only to provide an example that the rest of the world would do well to emulate.

Even so, from the first the idea of mission held within itself an impulse toward expansion. Americans, partly because they lacked ancient racial or ethnic ties to one another, began early to look elsewhere for a definition of national identity. They forged their bonds of unity from the ore of shared beliefs and experiences. To be an "American" was to believe in freedom and the Constitution, to work with others to clear the wilderness and build railroads across the prairies. While to be a Swede was just that—a concept that had little application in, say, Chile or Japan—to be an "American," an advocate of liberty and conqueror of nature, stood for things that might be relevant anywhere in the world. This missionary nationalism at first produced little more than a swaggering diplomatic posture, but as the nation grew in real power, Americans grew more confident of their superiority over others and the profoundly imperialistic implications of the American Mission began to emerge.

Isolationism. This diplomatic tradition, much misunderstood today, had an obvious meaning to Americans a century ago. At a time when the quickest passage from New York to London was 7½ days (record time) and from New York to Hong Kong was 120 days, Americans were ever mindful that their country was physically isolated from European power politics. But isolation was more than a physical fact; it was a national goal, and in two different senses. To the diplomatist, disentanglement from remote European affairs was a prudent way to advance selfish national interests. And to many Americans, isolation was an essential shield against contamination from decadent European mores and institutions.

Not that Americans were ever able to isolate themselves from the rest of the world. The United States conducted normal diplomatic and trade relations with other countries, often disregarded the doctrine of isolationism in Far Eastern affairs, and ignored it repeatedly in the Western Hemisphere. The generation of the Founding Fathers had hoped America would conduct commercial relations with all nations but establish political ties with none, and, although this goal was increasingly unrealizable (Felix Gilbert, *To the Farewell Address: Ideas of Early American Foreign Policy*, [1961]), its influence persisted in the form of staunch resistance to direct involvement in purely European political affairs. In this form the isolationist tradition retained vital strength and was perfectly expressed by Secretary of State Thomas F. Bayard in 1885: "So long as I am head of this Department, I shall not give myself the slightest trouble to thwart the small politics or staircase intrigues in Europe, in which we have not the slightest share or interest, and upon which I look with impatience and contempt."

The Monroe Doctrine. This operated in a sense as a corollary to isolationism, for it was only a small step from desiring noninterference within the hemisphere to insisting on it. Monroe's original statement in 1823 stipulated that Europeans should not reimpose their authority on already independent states in the hemisphere, but it did not demand the liberation of remaining European colonies. Nevertheless, underlying the doctrine was an implicit call for the eradication of all European influence in the area. Thus liberating Cuba ("get the Spanish out") or even annexing Canada ("get the British out") would seem appropriate ways to fulfill Monroe's dictum.

Actually it was not until 1895 during the Venezuela Crisis that the Monroe Doctrine was transformed from a timely policy for 1823 to a sacred principle for all time. Up till then the United States had applied the doctrine quite selectively, winking at those European incursions in the hemisphere that seemed harmless. On other occasions when such incursions were firmly resisted, the Monroe Doctrine itself was often not mentioned. But the idea of ridding the hemisphere of any *dangerous* European influence was gradually incorporated into American foreign policy in the years 1865–1900 and grew more attractive and urgent year by year.

The Open Door. Long before the Open Door notes of 1899–1900, Americans had used the phrase and recognized the importance of the policy it described. Decades before the depression of the mid-nineties and the panicky rush to export surplus industrial products, American businessmen had sought an open door for trade. This was true not only of exporters, who wanted low and nondiscriminatory tariffs for their goods (as well as other "open door" arrangements), but also import merchants bent on promoting an atmosphere conducive to maximum commercial traffic and shippers who profited from free and open ports around the world regardless of the point of origin of the goods carried in their vessels. Though the conduct of trade was generally considered a private matter, American statesmen from John Jay to John Hay had taken it for granted that one of their responsibilities was to facilitate the open door for American businessmen.

CONFLICTING INTERPRETATIONS

While few historians would differ with the discussion thus far, many issues in this period have been the subject of a multitude of conflicting interpretations. These conflicts pose no great problem for the specialist, who is equipped to sort out the contradictory material in his own field, but they often prove confusing to the average reader. It is hoped that the remainder of this chapter will dispel some of the confusion by examining closely five of the most important general issues that divide scholarly opinion on the subject of U.S. foreign relations from 1865 to 1900. Though these issues overlap at many points with one another, they are separated here for the sake of clarity into: (1) the Continuity Issue; (2) the Realism Issue; (3) the Economic Issue; (4) the Semantic Issue; and (5) the Deliberateness Issue.

The Continuity Issue. The question is whether American imperialism in the 1890s represented, on the one hand, a logical culmination of the preceding era or, on the other, a break with the past. Until the end of the 1950s most historians held to a "discontinuity" thesis. They argued that for twenty-five years after the Civil War Americans were too busy recovering from the conflict, settling the trans-Mississippi West, and building the most productive factories in the world to give much thought to foreign affairs. Though the Department of State did not shut its doors, it sought little more than to keep the United States out of trouble and protect its most obvious and nearby interests. Some Americans disapproved of even this minimal action, like the congressman who, during a budget debate in 1878, proposed that the United States maintain only two ministers abroad, one in London and the other in Berlin. Then, in sudden and rapid succession around 1890, intellectuals such as Josiah Strong, Brooks Adams, and Alfred T. Mahan began thinking imperialist thoughts, the construction of a modern fleet got underway, manufacturers started to clamor for foreign markets, and warmongering sensationalists captured the American press. Soon the United States was bullying Chile over a trivial incident, angling to annex Hawaii and Samoa, demanding a showdown with Great Britain over a South American border dispute, and ultimately seizing an overseas empire from Spain.

Some "discontinuity" historians have regarded the outburst of the nineties as the beginning of a long career of American imperialism in Asia and the Caribbean, while others have viewed it as an aberration followed by a return to nonimperialistic normality. But all agree that the outburst was a sharp break with the preceding diplomatic era when, as Henry Cabot Lodge complained in 1889, "our relations with foreign nations . . . fill but a slight place in American politics, and excite generally only a languid interest."

The "continuity" thesis, on the other hand, is most emphatically advanced by those historians who emphasize the economic foundations of diplomacy after the Civil War. The leading exponent of this view is Walter LaFeber, author of *The New Empire: An Interpretation of American Expansion, 1860–1898* (1963), who treats the latter part of the nineteenth century as a seamless epoch dominated throughout its length by America's transformation from an agrarian to an industrial nation. This transformation was accompanied by recurrent economic depressions, thought to be caused by industrial overproduction, which LaFeber sees as the dominant factor in U.S. foreign policy during the era. Unless the rapidly accumulating economic surplus could be marketed abroad, American society would face falling profits, mass unemployment, the rise of radical economic nostrums, and the possible collapse of middle-class democratic government itself. Thus, from Lincoln to McKinley, one administration after another employed foreign policy as an instrument for getting rid of this troublesome surplus (though the earlier administrations had not considered this as urgent a task as their successors). In LaFeber's view, the most significant break in continuity was a shift in tactics, but not objectives. This shift involved a change from the traditional assumption that America's economic goals could be achieved without the annexation of colonies, to the belief that colonialist solutions would be required after all. Reluctantly made and temporary in duration, the shift had several causes: the depression of the mid-nineties, which made the acquisition of new foreign markets more imperative than ever; the carving-up of China and soaring tariff walls of Europe, which threatened previously opened markets; and the unpredictable course of events during the Spanish-American War. But, though the tactics might alter, the essential strategy remained the same: sell off the destabilizing surplus of the American economy. (This argument was originally advanced by William A. Williams in *The Tragedy of American Diplomacy* [2d rev. ed., 1972], which concentrates on the period since the 1890s, and was incorporated in Williams's view of the broad sweep of history in *The Contours of American History* [1961], and further refined in his *The Roots of the Modern American Empire* [1969]; Thomas J. McCormick applies the thesis more narrowly to the background and development of John Hay's Open Door policy in *China Market: America's Quest for Informal Empire* [1967].)

Nearly all historians have detected some discontinuity in this period; the questions are: how much and how significant is it? Chronological watersheds of all sorts can be discovered, depending on the interests of the exploring historian. Events emphasized by one may be totally ignored by another. A "discontinuity" historian interested in demonstrating the suddenness of the imperialist surge of 1898–1900, for example, can point out that only three years earlier, in 1895, Secretary of State Walter Q. Gresham had said complacently of the Sino-Japanese War that it "endangers no policy of the United States in Asia." A "continuity" historian, on the other hand, might counter with evidence of how close the United States had come to war with Spain under Gresham's chief, President Cleveland, several years before the supposed watershed date of 1898. Still another historian, interested in applying the continuity-vs.-discontinuity test to American policy in various parts of the world in the years 1865 to 1900, might conclude that continuity prevailed in Europe and Africa, that a major change in relations with Latin America took place in 1895, if not earlier; and that the character of U.S. relations with East Asia was radically altered in 1898–1900. Thus the variations seem endless, but since many of the currently popular chronological frameworks are at least partially unsatisfactory, an attempt will be made to offer a new one later on in this book.

The Realism Issue. Nearly twenty-five years ago, in what turned out to be an extraordinarily influential book (*U.S.*

Diplomacy, 1900–1950 [1951]), diplomat and historian George F. Kennan indicted American foreign policy since the 1890s for its lack of realism. The idealism, moralism, and legalism that characterized American diplomacy produced costly failures that a single-minded advancement of selfish national interests would have avoided. Hans J. Morgenthau also advocated conducting U.S. foreign policy in a strict spirit of national self-interest and referred on occasion in historical passages to the gradual deterioration of American diplomacy since the "realistic" age of Hamilton and Washington (see *Politics Among Nations: The Struggle for Power and Peace* [1948 and later editions]; and *In Defense of the National Interest* [1951]). And historian Norman A. Graebner argued in his massive compendium of annotated documents, *Ideas and Diplomacy: Readings in the Intellectual Tradition of American Foreign Policy* (1964), that not only Hamilton and Washington but all eighteenth- and nineteenth-century American statesmen pursued policies that were "analytical" (his substitute for the overworked "realistic") until 1898, when they adopted a dangerous "ideological" policy in order to further American "political, social, and religious beliefs" instead of national "interests." The problem with American foreign policy since 1898 was, in short, the abandonment of "realism" for what Charles A. Beard once called a policy of "moral obligation, self-imposed. . . ."

Unfortunately, the issue as posed is imprecise at best. "Moralistic," "legalistic," "idealistic," "ideological," or "sentimental" are all extremely broad terms. And they are in no way synonymous. The concept of "realism" raises similar problems, for one man's realism is another's emotional spree. The historian who calls one action "realistic" and another "idealistic" is inescapably airing his own prejudices. Firm definitions of "realism" and "idealism" are illusive because individual and subjective considerations are always getting in the way and blurring the issue.

In any case, even if we accept the usefulness of the terms for the moment, a close look at American diplomacy in the latter part of the nineteenth century does not reveal any clear-cut "realistic" or "idealistic" pattern. Both labels can be applied. Certainly Secretary of State Frederick T. Frelinghuysen was being a realist in 1882 when he patiently explained to an overzealous American representative in Chile that any attempt to prevent war between Chile and Peru might require using United States forces, which was unthinkable since it would involve taxing Americans "for the exclusive benefit of foreign nations." But it was ideology pure and simple that prompted the United States to be the first country to recognize the Third French Republic in 1870 (as it had been the first to recognize the Second Republic in 1848), and it was ideology of a different sort that led James G. Blaine to say in 1889 that inter-American affairs should encompass no "artificial balance of power like unto that which has led to wars abroad and drenched Europe in blood." And, though a small point, what of Blaine's suggestion, ideological if anything ever was, that President Benjamin Harrison should avoid such words as *gracious, very gracious,* and *gratefully* in his speeches on the grounds that they smacked too much of British royalty?

Neither will the evidence support the thesis that American statesmen were all converted to dewy-eyed sentimentality after 1898. In 1898 Secretary of State William R. Day denied that the United States had a "humanitarian" duty to liberate Filipinos from Spanish rule, remarking skeptically: "Because we had done good in [Cuba], we were not therefore compelled to rush over the whole civilized world, six thousand miles away from home, to undertake tasks of that sort among people about whom we know nothing, and with whom we had no relations." His successor, John Hay, was also unsentimental. Though his Open Door notes of 1899–1900 have often been condemned as deluded attempts to solve major world problems with the immaterial force of rhetoric, he entertained no such illusions himself and once remarked to an associate that newspaper talk "about 'our pre-eminent moral position giving us authority to dictate to the world' is mere flap-doodle."

Terms like "realism" and "idealism" may be useful in differentiating such contrasting foreign policy figures as Alexander Hamilton and Woodrow Wilson, but they offer scant insight into most problems of American diplomatic historiography. The Realism Issue, when all is said and done, may only divert time and attention from more real and meaningful ones.

The Economic Issue. In contrast, an extremely vital issue among historians today, one which deserves extensive consideration, is the role of economic factors in late-nineteenth-century American foreign policy. For many years historians were influenced by writers like Julius W. Pratt (*Expansionists of 1898: The Acquisition of Hawaii and the Spanish Islands* [1936]), who demonstrated widespread business opposition to the decision to go to war in 1898, and other researchers who emphasized Social Darwinist ideology, yellow journalism, and popular frenzy as the prime causes of the Spanish-American War. As a result, they generally discounted the influence of economics on U.S. foreign policy in this era. But since the early 1960s, spearheaded by the works of Walter LaFeber and William A. Williams already discussed, an economic interpretation of the period has become widely accepted. It is, moreover, the only interpretive theory that purports to explain the meaning and significance of the entire period considered in this book.

An economic interpretation of American expansionism goes back at least as far as the Englishman John Hobson, who argued in *Imperialism* (1902) that the origins of this impulse were to be found in the efforts of moneylenders to find profitable new areas in which to invest their surplus capital. But the idea that J. P. Morgan singlehandedly got the United States ensconced in Manila has always been too much to swallow, and American historians—aware that the United States was a net borrower of capital until World War I—have tended to emphasize the search for foreign markets for goods, not capital, as the economic impetus to American imperialism. The search was necessary, according to this argument, because American industrialization had led to a productive surplus that must be disposed of abroad if businessmen were to avoid the unpleasant alternatives: decreased production, which would reduce profits and increase unemployment and social unrest, or, worse still because it reeked of socialism, a redistribution of wealth on a scale to permit lower-wage workers to buy the surplus products themselves.

Since neither alternative was attractive, another path was chosen—the government would help businessmen sell their surplus in other parts of the world. Thus, in this view, America's policymakers began the process of shaping U.S. diplomacy to these economic ends, haltingly at first right after the Civil War, but more systematically later on when business effectively supplanted agriculture as the dominant political influence in Washington and the need for action became more obvious. The climax came in the mid-nineties, precipitated by a shattering panic and depression and the news of the apparent disappearance of America's safety-valve frontier (Frederick Jackson Turner, "The Significance of the Frontier in American History," *Annual Report of the American Historical Association for the Year 1893*). These blows fell on an already unnerved population that had been nurtured on the story that America's progress would be onward-and-upward-forever. The threats of recurrent crisis or stagnation somehow had to be avoided, and an aggressive search for new markets seemed to provide the way out.

Latin America and the Far East were considered especially suitable areas for the construction of escape routes. Administrations once depicted as presenting a record of unparalleled mediocrity were actually, so the argument goes, establishing a crucial foundation for future developments by using tariff reform, reciprocity agreements, antirevolutionary and anti-European interventions, and other means to insure the increase of American exports. That the process culminated in war and the consequent acquisition of an empire did not mean that American leaders wanted it that way; it meant only that in 1898–99 they saw no other way to get what they did want without adopting such drastic methods.

This economic interpretation of the foreign policy of the period is not burdened with the cruder aspects of "left wing" history that have always been so easy to criticize. Such present-day exponents as Williams, LaFeber, and Thomas J.

McCormick have not made the mistake of blaming American imperialism on Wall Street or attributing it to some kind of conspiracy but have argued instead that American foreign policy was the product of a consensus of businessmen, politicians, and intellectuals. They do not brand these men as ideological colonialists, but rather as individuals who, if events had gone the way they hoped, would gladly have settled for a few small island bases of use to American merchants and the navy assigned to protect their trade. The leaders of the United States wanted an "informal empire" created by the demand for American products, not a formal empire dependent on the weapons of war.

Critics of this line of argument are quick to point out the apparently meager results of commercial diplomacy. Although U.S. exports to China rose from $3 million in 1890 to $15 million in 1900, the latter figure represented only 1.1 percent of total American exports, hardly an imperial proportion. It has also been noted that only a small portion of the gross national product in the late nineteenth century was involved in foreign trade, that most of this modest portion was with Canada and Europe and little with the "imperial" areas of Asia and Latin America (e.g., in 1900 about 44 percent of all U.S. exports went to Great Britain and France, while 3 percent went to China and Japan), and that agricultural rather than manufactured products continued to account for the bulk of American exports to the very end of the century.

"Informal empire" historians have made a three-fold response to these criticisms. First, they assert that American trade statistics of the time are not as modest and unimportant as they appear at first glance. Relatively small percentage increases in exports could make the difference between stagnation and prosperity, both for an individual company and the economy at large. For some industries exports to particular regions were crucial; almost 50 percent of the exports of the American cotton textile industry, for example, were shipped to China in the late 1890s. Second, they argued that their thesis does not depend upon massive economic results, but evidence that American leaders *believed* in the urgency of increased exports and the shimmering China market. Third, William A. Williams, in *Roots of the Modern American Empire*, has met the agricultural issue head-on. He points out himself that Americans earned as much in 1869 from the export of animal tallow and butter as from iron and steel, evidence of the continuing vitality of trade in agricultural commodities. Giving this fact its due attention, he concludes that the American obsession with exports started in Jeffersonian times; that wheat farmers, cattle-raisers, cotton farmers, dairymen, food processors, and others in the agricultural sector long pushed for a commercially oriented foreign policy; but that at the end of the century "metropolitan" business and political leaders took control of the export drive and turned it to the needs of an industrial economy. Thus Williams makes a valiant attempt to incorporate both preindustrial pressures for foreign markets and the continuing importance of agricultural exports in his economic interpretation of late-nineteenth-century U.S. diplomacy. And, by focusing attention once more on ordinary farmers and their spokesmen instead of the industrial-political elite, he places renewed emphasis on the popular roots of American imperialism.

The economic approach to American foreign policy from 1865 to 1900 contains many strong points and has found widespread acceptance, in part because of its appeal to the numerous critics of contemporary American foreign policy. But though it is valuable in explaining some specific episodes, this view has serious shortcomings as a key to the whole period. Not only is it simplistic to suppose there was a generation of policymakers invariably motivated by rational and precise calculations of the nation's economic interests, but a thorough sifting of the evidence turns up far too many discrepancies for an endorsement of the economic interpretation.

Much evidence, in fact, points in contrary directions. In 1870 when Secretary of State Fish put before the Grant cabinet a dispatch urging a concerted effort to increase American trade and influence in Hawaii, he was met with total silence and "the subject [was] dropped." In the same era the United States willingly jeopardized prospects for important new trade with China because of hostility at home to Chinese immigrants. No one was more eager for the China trade than Californians, yet, as Alexander DeConde states in his useful textbook, *A History of American Foreign Policy* (2d ed., 1971), "they were willing to sacrifice benefits that trade would bring rather than continue to accept the Chinese." Jobs and racial tensions were more important issues than foreign markets. In 1884 the Arthur administration actively participated in the Berlin conference on the Congo, from which many trade benefits were expected to flow; but the incoming Cleveland administration withdrew the conference treaty from the Senate in 1885 because it conflicted with American isolation from Big Power affairs, a tradition more deep-rooted than the imperatives of foreign trade. Did President Harrison shake the mailed fist at Chile in 1891–92 (Chapter Four) to open it up as a market for Connecticut locomotives, or was it to avenge an insult to the American uniform and counterbalance Great Britain's considerable influence in the Latin republic? The fact is that patriotic concerns and fear of European political influence in the hemisphere weighed more in Harrison's mind than commercial ledger sheets. James G. Blaine's vain attempt in 1881 to establish a Pan-American conference is often cited as a pioneering venture in market expansionism, but according to Russell H. Bastert he acted "from a mixture of many motives, probably least of all economic." His desire to be president was perhaps the most important ("A New Approach to the Origins of Blaine's Pan-American Policy," *Hispanic American Historical Review*, XXXIX, August 1959). Grover Cleveland's attempt to lower the tariff during the nineties was not a depression-induced maneuver to stimulate trade but the fulfillment of a political pledge he had made in 1887. He was responding to old Democratic party traditions and the ire of American consumers, not the needs of eastern industrialists (Paul S. Holbo, "Economics, Emotion, and Expansion: An Emerging Foreign Policy," in H. Wayne Morgan, ed., *The Gilded Age* [rev. ed., 1970]). Indeed, despite the calamitous depression of the nineties and the purported "consensus" on the wisdom of supporting all measures that would encourage exports, Congress quashed reciprocity agreements with Brazil, the Central American States, the British West Indies, Austria-Hungary, Germany, and Spain (involving Cuba and Puerto Rico). America's legislators apparently had not gotten the word.

One reason politicians did not take the foreign trade problem too seriously was that businessmen themselves set a bad example. Expansionist Brooks Adams complained bitterly of their "failure . . . to act intelligently and aggressively" in foreign markets. Milton Plesur has argued (*America's Outward Thrust: Approaches to Foreign Affairs, 1865-1890* [1971]) that American trade suffered constantly from plain old sloppiness and ineptitude in business practices—sending products abroad that were not only inferior, poorly packaged, and inappropriate for their designated markets, but in some cases unsafe as well (e.g., celluloid collars and cuffs made of harmful ingredients); poor timing (fur coats sent to Canada in July); and reliance upon incompetent or negligent local representatives. The general problem described by Plesur applied doubly in China, where commercial aspirations were supposedly greatest of all at the end of the century (Paul A. Varg, "The Myth of the China Market, 1890-1914," *American Historical Review*, LXXIII, February 1968). One historian notes that despite the urging of American political officials for special attention to be paid to area conditions, U.S. manufacturers "were slow to meet the trade demands of the Asian market" and "made little effort" to adapt their products to its needs (Marilyn B. Young, "American Expansion, 1870-1900: The Far East," in Barton J. Bernstein, ed., *Towards a New Past: Dissenting Essays in American History* [1968]; Young develops her argument more fully in *Rhetoric of Empire: American China Policy, 1895-1901* [1968]).

It is therefore highly misleading to think in terms of a unified American business community, backed by a determined government, striving unremittingly to break into the markets of Asia and Latin America. Most exporters still regarded trade as a matter between businessmen in any case; and of those who did believe that the government should have an active economic policy, most had in mind the protection of *home* markets by a high tariff wall, a strategy not designed to promote exports either in theory or practice. Protectionist sentiment remained intact throughout the Johnson-McKinley years, and free-trade views virtually disappeared from the expansionist Republican Party. Paul Holbo has pointed out that the annual debates in Congress on the tariff, far more passionate and rhetorical over the years than those aroused by foreign trade, spent their strength in arguments about workingmen's jobs, relief for consumers, and such ideological labels as "Americanism" and "Jeffersonianism" —not export strategy; and Tom E. Terrill, while generally supporting the economic interpretation, makes clear in *The Tariff, Politics, and American Foreign Policy, 1874–1901* (1973) how hard it was to turn attention from protection of the home market to expansion of foreign trade. As to the businessmen who were vitally interested in foreign sales, the great majority directed their attention to the profitable markets of Canada and Europe and failed to concentrate significantly on the undeveloped markets of Asia and Latin America until the era of Theodore Roosevelt and Woodrow Wilson (David E. Novack and Matthew Simon, "Commercial Responses to the American Export Invasion, 1871–1914: An Essay in Attitudinal History," *Explorations in Entrepreneurial History*, 2d ser., III, Winter 1966).

The behavior of American officials and businessmen does not support the carefully measured, symmetrical case put forward by LaFeber, Williams, McCormick, et al. That the United States government should skillfully and knowingly formulate and execute a farsighted economic foreign policy flies in the face of evidence that most American "policymakers," at least until the nineties, were amateurish and often maladroit in their diplomatic conduct, ignorant of and not particularly interested in the affairs of other nations, and much more inclined to react in the accustomed way to outside events than to initiate well-defined new policies. Behavior, not occasional rhetoric, is the crucial test. What, in actual fact, did presidents

and secretaries of state do through most of the years from 1865
to 1900? They revealed some interest in the expansion of foreign
markets, of course, but they also revealed much faintheartedness
or unconcern about such matters and consistently appointed to
the field men who were poorly qualified for any grand economic
promotional task. And Congress? It raised the tariff and rejected
the principle of reciprocal trade treaties, sacrificed quality in the
diplomatic service on the altar of thrift, and repeatedly put
partisan concerns high above good relations with other nations.
And businessmen? They concentrated overwhelmingly on sell-
ing to the ever-enlarging domestic market, and, when they did
get into the export game, continued to look to the traditional
and nonimperialistic markets of neighboring Canada and Europe. Tables I and II illustrate both points.

TABLE I

UNITED STATES EXPORTS AS PERCENTAGE OF ESTIMATED GROSS NATIONAL PRODUCT IN SELECTED YEARS

Year	Total Exports	Pct. of GNP (est.)
1874	$ 606,000,000	8.1%
1884	752,600,000	7.1
1889	762,700,000	6.4
1891	909,800,000	6.7
1893	862,300,000	6.5
1895	807,500,000	5.8
1897	1,051,000,000	7.5
1899	1,227,000,000	6.9
1900	1,394,500,000	7.5

This criticism does not mean the economic interpretation
should be rejected out of hand, but it must be blended where
possible with other views to create a useful synthesis. Historians
have always noted, of course, that foreign trade and other
economic factors have been important in American diplomacy.

TABLE II

EXPORTS TO CANADA AND EUROPE COMPARED WITH EXPORTS TO ASIA AND LATIN AMERICA

Year	Exports to Canada and Europe	Pct. of Total	Exports to Asia and Latin America	Pct. of Total
1875	$ 494,000,000	86.1%	$ 72,000,000	12.5%
1885	637,000,000	85.8	87,000,000	11.7
1895	681,000,000	84.3	108,000,000	13.4
1900	1,135,000,000	81.4	200,000,000	14.3

Tables compiled from information in *Historical Statistics of the United States,* 1960; U.S. Department of Commerce, *Long Term Growth, 1860–1965,* 1966; National Bureau of Economic Research, *Trends in the American Economy in the Nineteenth Century,* 1960.

The problem has been that few writers, including the recent revisionists, have integrated these factors into a general framework or emphasized their significant political and ideological overtones. Agile politicians throughout the years have manipulated these economic currents for their own purposes; David Healy has argued that many statesmen with power and prestige uppermost in their minds used a rhetoric heavily dosed with "markets" talk to win support from a public more concerned with dollars and cents than glory (*US Expansionism: The Imperialist Urge in the 1890s* [1970]). Even more common than politicians who manipulated economic, political, and ideological issues were those who never dreamed of separating them. They might, for example, have wanted to increase American political influence in China during the 1890s, but for what purpose if not to open doors for U.S. exports? Or, conversely, they might have wanted to increase exports as a means of enhancing American political influence throughout the Far East.

In short, as Marilyn B. Young has written, most Americans merged economics into a broader view "which saw a strong navy, trade, political power, and the territory necessary . . . to maintain both trade and power, as complementary factors contributing to the wealth and strength of the nation." Moreover, since the time of the Revolution, Americans have considered foreign trade to be not only a source of money profits, but a wellspring of social enlightenment and a beneficent bond between distant peoples (James A. Field, Jr., *America and the Mediterranean World, 1776–1882* [1969]). Foreign commerce was, in addition, a source of American pride; Paul A. Varg observes that it "flattered the ego of Americans to think of their country as the supplier of the world's market. . . ." Thus American interest in foreign trade has long transcended exclusively economic horizons, a fact that must be understood if we are properly to appreciate the actual role of economics in late-nineteenth-century American foreign policy.

The Semantic Issue. A common source of confusion, but one that need not detain us long, is the word "imperialism" as applied to American diplomacy from 1865 to 1900. Most Americans have interpreted the word in narrow terms to mean only the formal annexation and control of other territories and peoples. In fact, they have sometimes avoided applying the word to American actions that appear to meet even this narrow definition. The seizure of the Southwest from Mexico, for example, was not "imperialistic" because the territory was previously uninhabited (except, of course, for some tens of thousands of Indians and Mexicans who didn't count) and was eventually incorporated into the Union as states. Nor was the annexation of Puerto Rico "imperialistic" because the local populace did not resist the takeover; nor that of the Philippines, where the natives did resist but were treated benevolently after succumbing and finally let go. If such distortions of language stem from hypersensitive American pride, a recent hypercritical assessment of the American experience has so vulgarized "imperialism" as to make it almost useless in rational discourse. What can the word possibly mean when it is pasted as a label everywhere the United States has troops stationed abroad, U.S. citizens have invested money, or foreigners drink Coke?

Since the word "imperialism" generates so much more heat

than light today, it is especially fortunate that some historians are trying to use it and related terms much more precisely than in the past. Marilyn B. Young, for instance, distinguishes between "annexationists, mild or extreme," and those who "advocated expanding foreign markets through forceful diplomatic representation, the reform of the consular service, and the construction of an isthmian canal." Most members of the new "economic school" go to great lengths to distinguish among varying *isms*, generally arguing that most Americans were not "colonialists," who wanted to govern other peoples, but rather "expansionists," "open door expansionists," "informal imperialists," or "anticolonial imperialists." In one extraordinary sentence Thomas J. McCormick has rung all the changes, writing: "Paradoxically, American expansion was designed in part to serve an anti-imperial purpose of preventing the colonization of China and thus preserving her for open door market penetration: *the imperialism of anti-imperialism* ('neo-colonialism' in today's parlance.)"

That explosion of terminology suggests that the wisest course is to acknowledge the difficulty of formulating precise definitions acceptable to all parties, use the terms concerned clearly but pragmatically, and recognize that different groups of men advocated the different "policies" which have been so variously labeled. At least six species of *Imperialistus americanus* can be discerned among the fauna of late-nineteenth-century American history (along with many hybrid combinations): (1) The Market Expansionist, pure and simple, who wanted nothing more than to empty the warehouse of America's productive surplus; (2) The Market Expansionist, subspecies A, who wanted to buttress his export campaign with a strong navy, and to strengthen the navy by acquiring island "dots" and "points" useful as harbors, coaling stations, and repair facilities; (3) The Market Expansionist, subspecies B, who was prepared to go one step further and accept the burden of direct colonial rule over other peoples, but only if absolutely necessary to maintain influence in areas strategically important to the United States; (4) The Power Politician, who hailed the rising international power of the United States, wished to see the ascent continue for its own sake, and to that end was willing to use a variety of instruments, including commercial diplomacy and colonialism; (5) The Colonialist, whose main interest lay in seizing the opportunity to govern less developed peoples so that America could "civilize" them, bringing them the Word of God and initiating them in the wondrous workings of Anglo-Saxon political institutions; (6) The Wild Jingo, like Benjamin F. Butler, who once urged expansion "so far north that wandering Esquimau will mistake the flashings of the midnight sun reflected from our glorious flag for the scintillations of an *aurora borealis.*" Allan Nevins has described an earlier phase of this last-mentioned spirit with the felicitous phrase, "Davy Crockett spread-eaglism."

The Deliberateness Issue. This issue can be stated in the form of a question: Was American foreign policy from 1865 to 1900 made in a deliberate fashion, carefully conceived and systematically executed by men who knew what they were doing, or was it passive, reactive, and haphazardly administered by officials who lacked both reliable information and conscious policy designs? The economic-school revisionists, plus a group of historians convinced for other reasons that late-nineteenth-century America should be rescued from old stereotypes of venality and mediocrity, have generally argued the former, while other historians of various schools have favored the latter. The answer to this question is doubly significant because it determines in large part how we visualize the American diplomatic terrain of the period and, at the same time as we shall later see, suggests another way to interpret some major diplomatic changes of the nineties.

The strongest case in support of the systematic foreign policy theory has been made by advocates of the foreign-markets thesis, which presupposes consciousness of purpose on the part of American policymakers. We have already discussed this thesis, but there are many other examples of deliberateness in U.S. diplomacy worth our attention, including some not associated with commercialist policy. As many historians, most recently Ernest N. Paolino in *The Foundations of the American Empire: William Henry Seward and U.S. Foreign Policy* (1973), have made clear, Secretary of State William H. Seward had a profoundly ambitious vision of America's imperial future and an elaborate set of both domestic and international schemes for its fulfillment. His successor Hamilton Fish performed with impressive skill in 1869–71 when he expertly and simultaneously juggled three major issues—Grant's effort to annex the Dominican Republic, U.S. policy in the Cuban Rebellion, and the *Alabama* claims—and resolved them all to his satisfaction (Chapter Two). Regardless of whether one calls his effort skillful political infighting or something more flattering, it was remarkable nonetheless. James G. Blaine's foreign policy was usually more expedient than deliberate, but it was no political amateur who used the following words in 1881 to describe the commercial importance of forging closer ties with Hawaii:

Taking San Francisco as the commercial center on the western slope, a line drawn northwesterly to the Aleutian group marks our Pacific border almost to the confines of Asia. A corresponding line drawn southwesterly from San Francisco to Honolulu, marks the natural limit of the ocean belt within which our trade with the oriental countries must flow, and is, moreover, the direct line of communication between the United States and Australasia. Within this line lies the commercial domain of our western coast.

Historians have attributed to President Harrison a comprehensive understanding of the interlocking relationships that connect the naval, commercial, and diplomatic components of foreign policy; in recent years they have agreed that McKinley, traditionally regarded as an amiable weather vane, was an able president and steward of a systematic foreign policy. (Several of the "foreign-markets" thesis works already cited have boosted McKinley's reputation for intelligence and political skill. Others who have demonstrated considerable respect for McKinley, without placing a special emphasis on economics, include Margaret Leech, *In the Days of McKinley* [1959]; H. Wayne Morgan, in his *William McKinley and His America* [1963], and

America's Road to Empire: The War with Spain and Overseas Expansion [1965]; and Paul S. Holbo, "Presidential Leadership in Foreign Affairs: William McKinley and the Turpie-Foraker Amendment," *American Historical Review*, LXXII, July 1967.)

Some regions of the world seemed to inspire more consistent and coherent definitions of policy than others. In Latin America an entire generation of statesmen worked at reducing local European influence, promoting the peaceable settlement of regional disputes and the expanded sale of American goods, and securing U.S. control of a future isthmian canal. China, too, tended to call forth unusual deliberateness in United States policymaking, though not until the last five years of the century.

All the above is impressive, but not overpowering. The fact remains that many American officials were unsophisticated in world affairs, with an approach more chaotic than systematic. No matter how able, they normally waited inertly until an external stimulus of crisis proportions forced them to formulate a suitable American response. Despite sporadic gestures toward reform—and with some happy exceptions—the consular service was made up largely of unimaginative functionaries and hacks, bumptious fools, and petty corruptionists. Many did little besides complain to Washington about the meager allowance for furniture and the condition in which their predecessors had left the offices. The government sent them to their posts with minimal and uniform instructions that supposedly applied as well to Caracas as to Hamburg, Winnipeg, or Kobe. An 1872 report by a Special Inspector of American consular officials in Asia and South America concluded that "not a single consulate [had] a complete set of record-books . . . as required," and that "almost every consulate had some defects . . . owing to the incompetency, low habits, and vulgarity of some of its officers during the endless round of evils" caused by rapid turnover of personnel. "Abuses had been committed in the collection of fees; in the exercise of judicial powers; in the adjustment of the business affairs of American citizens; in the settlement, where permitted, of the estates of intestate American citizens dying abroad; . . . and issuing illegal passports; . . . [and] in taxing

Chinese emigrants," but the worst "iniquity" was "defrauding the government and grasping gains from various outside sources."

Aside from such able men as John A. Kasson, Charles Francis Adams, and John Hay, American ministers and ambassadors (a rank not used until 1893) all too often earned more shame than respect for their country. In an era when foreign envoys still had great influence in diplomacy, what can be said of a government that sent abroad men like Lewis D. Campbell, minister to republican Mexico in 1867, who wouldn't budge from his legation "headquarters" in New Orleans to deliver Seward's plea for the life of the fallen Emperor Maximilian; or the amazing Rumsey Wing of Kentucky, whom Grant sent at the age of twenty-seven to Ecuador, which he promptly urged the United States to annex, where he attempted to assassinate the British ambassador, and where he finally succumbed to dt's and fever; or Charles E. DeLong, who sent ungrammatical and misspelled dispatches to Secretary Fish and astonished the Japanese by careening through Tokyo streets at full speed in his carriage, his whip cracking at startled pedestrians and a pistol stuck prominently in his belt; or peg-legged Dan Sickles, sent to Spain in the 1870s, who purportedly made love to the Queen Regent and came close to making war during the Cuban Rebellion by forwarding to Washington *by mail* news conducive to peace and *by cable* news of an opposite sort; or the nephew of Ben Butler, U.S. Consul General in Egypt, whose recall was demanded after he was accused of heavy drinking, purchasing slave wenches, and participating in a wild shooting spree? Little wonder, as Milton Plesur relates, that the New York *Daily Tribune* suggested in 1886 that a commission of scientists experiment with balloons to ascertain how high in the heavens American diplomats could be sent "without disgracing themselves and their country."

Incompetence and amateurishness are not the only point. The United States may have had some kind of "policy" for China and Latin America, albeit in the latter case more negative than positive, but it had literally none for Europe, in the capitals of which American diplomats composed dispatches almost totally bereft of references to the Continent's shifting alliances and recurrent crises. The "Eastern Question," so worrisome to Europeans in the seventies and eighties, did not disturb the slumbers of American diplomats. Even with regard to Latin America, Washington left it up to its minister in Mexico City to decide whether to recognize the new Díaz regime in 1877, and in Asia during the nineties the government often acted passively, refusing a European invitation to join in mediating the Sino-Japanese War (1894-95), snubbing its minister to China when he urged a more forward policy, and shortly thereafter refusing to help American businessmen who complained of being cheated out of a chance to build a Peking-to-Hankow railroad. Not until 1899 did the United States take the initiative in China, and even then John Hay remarked that it was "not very easy to formulate with any exactness the view of the Government" on Chinese matters. When we recall that the day-to-day preoccupations of American diplomatic officials usually ran to protecting an errant missionary in Turkey or negotiating an extradition treaty with Russia rather than administering a "policy" or announcing a major "decision," we will avoid seeing too much deliberateness and consistency in post–Civil War American diplomacy.

Some Americans, of course, were well informed about world affairs and clear in their view of what U.S. policy should be, but such men—whether ministers, naval officers, international businessmen, or missionaries—normally operated on their own hook. Far ahead of their government, which responded infrequently if at all to their importunities, they occasionally achieved impressive advances for the United States—some of which were reluctantly sanctioned after the fact by Washington while others were allowed to lapse through official indifference and inaction. Robert Wiebe has observed that diplomatic initiatives usually originated elsewhere than in Washington, that American "foreign relations were composed of incidents, not policies—a number of distinct events, not sequences that moved from a source toward a conclusion" (*The Search for Order, 1877–1920* [1967]). This began to change in the 1890s, however, when the passivity and drift of American foreign policy started to give way to more deliberateness and consistency. We must now turn to this change and the reasons for its appearance.

TWO

Old Paradigm
Policy, 1865–1889

PARADIGMS AND DIPLOMACY

Historians have long noticed that in the fabric of late-nineteenth-century American foreign policy some patterns stand out in bold relief against a background of somber hues and random traceries. These patterns, visible to all, represent the era's most important developments: a growing American domination of the Caribbean, the introduction of a continuous U.S. interest and presence in East Asia, the aquisition of an extraterritorial empire, and the emergence of the United States as a major world power. But, as we have seen, observers have sharply disagreed on the chronology of these developments, the relative importance of economic factors in bringing them about, and the purposefulness of the government in shaping these new patterns of foreign policy.

We may be able to resolve some of these disagreements by recognizing that something quite *different* began to appear in U.S. diplomacy around 1890—the threads in the tapestry, though still intertwined and somewhat confused, began to sort themselves out and head off in new directions. The something that happened in the nineties was a major shift in the manner of thinking about and executing American foreign policy: the old reactive and unsystematic conduct of U.S. foreign relations was replaced by the formulation of a real "policy" in international affairs and its more-or-less systematic execution. Thus, hypothetically speaking, while a secretary of state in 1880 would probably have reacted separately and disjointedly to events in, say, Mexico, Canada, and China, his successor in 1900 would have anticipated the need for decision before events overtook him, perhaps pondered both events and decision in a framework calculated to advance a general foreign policy, and then acted accordingly.

This is not to say that American foreign policy underwent a 100 percent transformation in the decade before 1900; it did, however, change remarkably in some respects and actually began to change as early as the late 1880s. What we need is a new interpretive tool to explain these changes—not a grand theory, but a new way of thinking about this period of American diplomatic history that will reconcile, and when necessary refine, some of the major interpretations that already exist. Just such a helpful analytical tool is available in the "paradigm."

The word "paradigm" means model or pattern, but it takes on a special meaning in Thomas S. Kuhn's enormously suggestive book on the history of science, *The Structure of Scientific Revolutions* (2d ed., 1970)—a meaning that can usefully be applied to the field of diplomatic history, as we shall shortly see.

Kuhn uses paradigm to refer to an "entire constellation of beliefs, values, techniques," axioms, and theories shared by a community of scientists at any particular time in history. The belief that the sun revolved around the earth set one paradigm, and the Copernican "revolution" established another. Physicists who thought of electricity as a fluid conducted experiments and communicated with one another within the framework of one paradigm, while twentieth-century physicists operate within another. A paradigm determines the contemporary definitions of scientific "truth" and respectable scientific activity (astrology is not a respectable science in the 1970s, but it once was), establishes a scientific field's methodology and the "expectations" of its practitioners, and serves as a filter for the perception of evidence and generally defines the way a scientist sees the "objective" natural world around him.

When widespread disagreements divide scientists about the fundamentals of their field, no paradigm is in effect. Conversely, when a paradigm is in force, scientists consider the basic principles of their field as givens and are therefore free to concentrate on solving derivative problems in a kind of "mopping-up" operation, as Kuhn puts it. At such times communication among scientists is quick and simple since important words and formulas need only to be stated to be instantly recognized. A scientific paradigm in this sense is like "an accepted judicial decision in the common law," a general principle requiring only "further articulation and specification. . . ." Just as the judge quickly alludes for reference to a major precedent and then gets on with the work at hand, so the scientist makes a quick reference to "velocity" or "energy"—without fear of being misunderstood—and then concentrates on solving the special problem facing him.

According to Professor Kuhn, paradigms do not usually succeed one another gradually and incrementally, but abruptly. Scientists tend to remain stubbornly loyal to a paradigm—it is, after all, their definition of the real world—even when confronted with multiple discoveries contradicting it. These "anomalies," as Kuhn calls them, are first shrugged off as accidental quirks, or simply ruled out of order, but if they appear often enough to disrupt normal expectations and throw doubt on accepted procedures, the anomalies end up by creating "incommensurable ways of seeing the world and of practicing science in it"—in short, a scientific crisis. At this juncture, a new theory usually arises to explain the anomalies, reinterpreting them as "normal" occurrences and, as soon as enough scientists concur, rather suddenly takes over as the new paradigm. A "scientific revolution" will have occurred, after which, in a manner of speaking, scientists will be "responding to a different world."

Although Kuhn was writing about the history of science, Michael Roskin has profitably adapted his paradigm theory in an imaginative study of contemporary foreign policy ("Turning Inward: The Effects of the Vietnam War on U.S. Foreign Policy," Ph.D. dissertation, The American University, 1972); a further adaptation is suggested here as an aid in explaining the "revolution" in American foreign policy in the 1890s. The analogy to scientific change cannot be taken too literally, of course. The second of the two diplomatic "paradigms" discussed below, for example, did not succeed the first instantaneously or ever completely replace it. Compared to descriptions of clear-cut scientific revolutions, the picture of American diplomatic change is rather on the muddy side; instead of appearing full-blown overnight, the new paradigm gradually grew in strength and significance throughout the 1890s. And from approximately 1888 to 1895 the factors that caused the old paradigm to topple are sometimes hard to distinguish from the characteristics of its successor.

Nonetheless, an analogy need not be exact to be helpful, and it will be highly useful for the following reasons to think of American foreign policy from 1865 to 1900 as a period during which one paradigm supplanted another:

1. The concept of paradigm change is an excellent synthesizer that will reconcile certain interpretations normally considered irreconcilable by providing a new framework for looking at this period.

2. A theory of paradigmatic change helps to settle the

"discontinuity issue" by explaining some of the domestic and diplomatic shocks America sustained in the late eighties and early nineties, not as manifestations of slow, incremental change nor as expected ups-and-downs on a graph of normality, but as the kind of "anomalies" that establish the climate necessary for fundamental change.

3. It helps in making the subtle but important point that the new American foreign policy of the late 1890s was more than the sum of its individual components. American policymakers were, of course, responding to gradually changing conditions, but their view of those conditions was powerfully affected by new beliefs and assumptions on their part. The world as an historian would describe it might have changed only a little from 1875 to 1895, but to the American diplomat of 1895 the change would have seemed very great because of his own transformed perceptions—that is, because of the change in paradigms.

4. In emphasizing methods and procedures as well as goals and objectives, the paradigm theory has additional value in reminding us that the rise of imperialism was not the only important phenomenon of late-nineteenth-century American diplomacy. Important changes were simultaneously occurring in the way Americans thought about and conducted foreign policy. One such change was the shift from "incidents" to "policy," so ably discussed, as we have noted earlier, by Robert Wiebe.

5. Finally, by recognizing that the 1865–89 period, to which the rest of this chapter is devoted, was dominated by a paradigm of its own—instead of seeing it as either a preliminary stage of the "new empire" or a muddled epoch with no pattern whatever —we can, in a way quite different from other recent revisionists, reaffirm the historical integrity of the era. Instead of imposing on it a coherence that did not exist, or succumbing to the temptation of Gilded Age historians to satirize the era, we can say that, yes, the foreign policy of these years was often as meandering and erratic as traditionally described, but that, given the terms of the old paradigm, such a policy was perfectly coherent to Americans of the time.

What to call the two paradigms, overlapping with but

succeeding one another from about 1889 to the mid-nineties, presents something of a problem since one-word labels fail to do justice to their essential qualities. "Continental" might appear to fit the earlier paradigm, for instance, but its exclusive emphasis on geography suggests nothing about the manner and method of American foreign policy; "imperial" certainly suggests much of what was characteristic of the later paradigm, but it, too, fails to hint of the important change from "incidents" to "policy." Any pair of terms, to be acceptable as sufficiently descriptive, should suggest something about the content, geographical scope, manner, and method of American foreign policy. Since such precise terms are hard to come by, we will refer simply to the Old and New Paradigms.

How the Old Paradigm gave way to the New and what the latter consisted of in detail are discussed in the next chapter. Here we are concerned with the heyday of the Old Paradigm that extended, roughly speaking, from the end of the Civil War to the advent of the Harrison administration in 1889. These were years when the outlook of American policymakers was generally isolationist, noninterventionist, and unilateralist; their customary manner of conducting foreign affairs was passive and reactive, their guidance of diplomats sent abroad—many of whom were rank amateurs—was minimal and vague, and their country's army and navy were ill prepared for serious warfare. Congressmen of the time saw nothing amiss in using foreign policy to achieve partisan political ends, just as they used rivers-and-harbors bills or Indian agencies for the same purpose. High State Department officials spent little time defining U.S. "policy." All were in agreement—the core assumption of the Old Paradigm—that the United States was safe, her security threatened in no way by anyone.

THE *ALABAMA* CLAIMS AND MEXICO

In 1865 American officials were unable to avoid two explosive disputes that had arisen during the Civil War—one with Great

Britain, the other with France. Secretaries of State William H. Seward and Hamilton Fish handled the defusing of these disputes with skill and dispatch, but without the aid of a general policy. The problems were thrust upon them, they reacted to them, and then they sat back to see what would happen next—a perfect example of Old Paradigm behavior.

The more dangerous of the two disputes was the one with Great Britain. The United States had accused England of illegal pro-Confederate conduct that had injured the Union and prolonged the Civil War. Although she had respected the Union's blockade of Confederate ports, Britain's proclamation of neutrality in May 1861, which prompted similar declarations by other European governments, conferred on the South the coveted status of belligerent, including the right to raise loans and send diplomats abroad and attack Union commerce at sea. In 1862 the British stopped just short of the more fateful step of recognizing Southern independence and proposing international mediation of the war. In the meantime, British shipyards turned out powerful cruisers for the Confederacy, avoiding open violation of British neutrality laws by a series of flagrant subterfuges. Stern Union protests finally put an end to these sales in 1863—but too late to stop delivery of such rebel cruisers (mostly British-manned) as the *Alabama*, *Shenandoah*, and *Florida*, which destroyed or disabled about 250 Northern ships, wrecked the Pacific whaling fleet, raised maritime insurance rates to prohibitively high levels, and caused over 700 Yankee merchant ships to change to British registry for self-protection. Unable to act during the war, Seward grimly kept track of the record of damages.

Evidence of a retaliatory spirit appeared as early as 1864 when the United States gave notice (later rescinded) that it would abrogate the Rush-Bagot Treaty and thus free itself to increase armaments on the Great Lakes. In addition, Congress in 1865 terminated an eleven-year-old Canadian reciprocity treaty vital to Canada's prosperity and imposed stiff passport regulations on Canadian travelers, the House passed a new neutrality law in 1866 permitting Americans to construct warships for belligerents (raising the specter of future *Alabamas* cruising against British commerce), and in 1867 protested ominously against the unifying confederation of Canada. At any time during these years the *Alabama* claims could probably have been quickly settled had the British been willing to apologize. They let the opportunity pass, and the Americans grew angrier. Just how angry became evident in 1869 when the Senate rejected a hastily contrived settlement that was deemed too easy on the British—the Johnson-Clarendon Convention—by the stunning vote of 54–1.

Not only had the Senate apparently slammed the door on a moderate settlement, but Charles Sumner of Massachusetts, its greatest luminary in foreign affairs, had dramatically upped the ante in an electrifying speech. British misdeeds, he asserted, had caused $15 million in direct damages to American ships—a reasonable estimate. But, he added, John Bull was responsible for "indirect" or "national" damages, such as increased insurance rates, the loss of American merchant ships to British registry ($110 million for these two items), and compensation for goods never risked on the seas at all for fear of Confederate raids. Most important, he held Britain responsible for encouraging the rebels with her pro-Southern sympathies to such a degree that it doubled the length of the war, the total cost of which, by his estimate, was $4 billion. "Everybody can make the calculation," he said, but also implied that, in lieu of cash payment, the United States would graciously accept the gift of Canada!

Secretary of State Hamilton Fish, who inherited the problem just as his old friend Sumner was stirring up the muddy waters, wanted an amicable settlement. He had his work cut out for him. The noises from London remained as unrepentant as ever, and Grant, deliberate as a general but impulsive as a president, relished the idea of having Phil Sheridan march into Canada. Fish decided to wait for tempers to cool and events to move his way before resuming formal talks. Fortunately for him, they did: Grant broke with Sumner when the latter came out against the annexation of Santo Domingo, Fish gained a free hand in diplomacy through threats to resign, businessmen demonstrated an eagerness for accommodation, Republicans hankered for a positive achievement to offset growing criticism of the administration, and renewed disputes with Canada over fisheries grounds and the San Juan boundary in the Northwest reinforced the need for settlement. In addition, the public was shifting its attention to other issues. The clincher was probably the realization that Canadians overwhelmingly opposed American annexation, thus eliminating any obvious advantage to expansionists in prolonging the dispute.

At the same time, the British were moderating their position, in part because of difficulties in Europe that required full attention and a safe Atlantic flank. Talks on all outstanding Anglo-American issues finally got underway, at first in private and then in a Joint High Commission that convened in Washington early in 1871. In a pattern often repeated in the next thirty years, Britain had to lean heavily on Canada before the latter would agree to accords already agreed upon with the United States. But the Canadians did finally come around and sign the Treaty of Washington in May 1871. The San Juan dispute was submitted to German arbitration and later settled in favor of the United States. American fishing rights in Canadian waters were expanded in exchange for a *quid pro quo* for British subjects in American waters plus a cash award (settled upon in 1877) of $5.5 million to Canada. The St. Lawrence River was permanently opened to U.S. shipping and three major rivers in Alaska to Canadian vessels. As to the *Alabama* claims, Great Britain expressed her regret for the actions of the Confederate cruisers though she did not "apologize" or admit to acting illegally; it was further agreed that the figure for the damages should be determined by an arbitration tribunal in Geneva made up of representatives from Brazil, Italy, Switzerland, and the two contesting parties, with the stipulation that they make their decision according to standards of neutral conduct spelled out in the treaty in a way that guaranteed a settlement generally favorable to the United States. Nothing was said in the treaty about "indirect" claims, an issue the British were confident they had heard the last of. When the United States decided to reopen this issue in Geneva, not in hopes of collecting any money but of placating jingo critics at home and getting the issue settled once and for all in international law, the British felt they had been betrayed by a shrewd Yankee trick. The whole agreement might have come unglued if Charles Francis Adams, the American member of the Geneva tribunal, had not dreamed up a facesaving formula for all parties: the arbitrators announced that they had taken solemn notice of the indirect claims (which satisfied the Americans) but had not found them deserving of official consideration (which mollified the British). The five-man body was then free to complete its work in September of 1872 with an award of $15.5 million to the United States for direct damages. The process of painstaking discussion and compromise known as "diplomacy" had settled a serious international conflict, and bows were in order to all concerned.

The second important dispute left in the wake of the Civil War, though not as dangerous or resistant to settlement as the *Alabama* claims, was the French establishment of their Hapsburg puppet, Ferdinand Maximilian, as emperor of Mexico. The project had originated in 1861 when France, Britain, and Spain sent a joint military expedition to collect debts repudiated by the Mexican Congress. The United States had warily turned down an invitation to join the expedition, supposedly only a routine debt-collecting enterprise. Britain and Spain withdrew from the venture when they realized that Napoleon III's real ambition was to establish in the New World a Catholic monarchy beholden to French power. Napoleon's intent was to gratify French Catholics, confound domestic critics with a little old-fashioned *gloire,* and check the expansion of American power. Despite stubborn resistance from the forces of Mexican President Benito Juarez, he gained full control of the country by 1864 and placed Maximilian and his ambitious empress Carlota on the ancient throne of Montezuma.

Preoccupied by the Union military defeats of 1861–62, Secretary of State Seward politely registered American displeasure and bided his time, but he began to exert more pressure as Northern victories mounted and domestic hostility to Napoleon grew. The United States refused to break off diplomatic relations with Juarez's guerrilla regime and stepped up the frequency of its messages of displeasure to Paris. In 1864 the House of Representatives unanimously demanded French withdrawal and, with the Civil War at an end, 50,000 battle-tested bluecoats under General Sheridan stood poised on the Mexican border. The mouse might play while the cat was away, but now the cat was back.

If President Andrew Johnson had followed General Grant's suggestion, the rough stuff might have started immediately, but Secretary of State Seward adroitly mapped his own course, firmly urging Napoleon to remove his troops while politely holding the door open for their departure. Believing that Maximilian would in all likelihood be toppled by growing resistance in Mexico, Seward never demanded that the puppet Empire be dismantled or waved the Monroe Doctrine in Napoleon's face, but insisted only that French troops leave Mexico. At first the French offered to withdraw troops in exchange for U.S. recognition of Maximilian; Seward responded by sending a new minister to Juarez's government. Napoleon saw the game was up when Britain turned down a French bid for help and Seward demanded on February 12, 1866, a specific date for withdrawal. His adventure had become unpopular at home, and his troops were needed for contingencies in Europe. In April 1866 France announced its imminent withdrawal; the last soldier left a year later. The Empire collapsed, and Maximilian was captured and executed after scorning chances to escape. One of many tragedies for the Hapsburg family, the Mexican affair was, for the United States, a major victory in the power struggle for the Western Hemisphere (the most recent account is to be found in Alfred J. and Kathryn A. Hanna, *Napoleon III and Mexico: American Triumph over Monarchy* [1971]).

SEWARD, GRANT, AND BLAINE

In the *Alabama* and Mexico affairs no general "policy" was pursued; Seward and Fish merely dealt with immediate and unavoidable pressures in approved Old-Paradigm style. Some historians believe, however, that a consistent and purposeful drive toward empire began to emerge immediately after the Civil War—that the New Paradigm, as we are calling it, arrived on the scene long before the nineties. Prominently associated with this alleged early surge of deliberate expansionism are Seward's post–Civil War years as secretary of state (1865–69), the period of the Grant administration (1869–77), and James G. Blaine's brief first term as secretary of state (1881). These cases require our attention before we can go on to a description of other important diplomatic developments in the years 1865 to 1889.

Of the three, Seward's case is the most intriguing because he was, in fact, the author of an elaborate imperial design that he held consistently through several decades. As he saw it, history, Providence, and commercial and strategic necessity all pointed toward an imperial future for the United States. The locus of the world's great empires had been moving westward for many centuries; now America, with God's sanction, was at the center of power; it must follow its mandatory course into the Pacific and Asia if it was to enjoy continued economic development and security from Old World rivals. To make the home base strong for external expansion, Seward prescribed high tariffs, cheap land and labor, and efficient transportation to speed up full internal development.

But his vision was not a prescription for specific action. Seward often sounded more like a spread-eagle jingo than an imperial policymaker; he declared in 1867 that, with continued peace at home and "fifty, forty, thirty more years of life," he would deliver to his country "the possession of the American continent and the control of the world." A haphazard hunger for glory lay behind his belief that the American Empire would eventually stretch from the Arctic Circle to Panama and have its capital in Mexico City; a crude greed, not painstaking diplomatic planning, lay behind his hope, expressed at various times, of acquiring not only Alaska and Midway, but Santo Domingo, Haiti, Martinique, the Virgin Islands, the Bahamas, Cuba, Puerto Rico (and the nearby uninhabited islands of Culebra and

Culebrita), St. Bartholomew's Island, Tiger Island (off the west coast of Central America), Hawaii, British Columbia, St. Pierre, Greenland, and Iceland. This was more like Theodore Roosevelt's biennial itch for "a war" than a carefully calculated policy, and it was aimed at shoring up the Johnson administration and perhaps making himself president as much as at any definite foreign policy goal.

Seward's record was nonetheless notable, quite apart from his skillful handling of Civil War diplomacy and the already-discussed Mexican affair. In addition to acquiring Alaska and supporting the navy's occupation of Midway Island in 1867, he joined European powers in sustaining Western treaty rights in Japan, concluded a commercial pact with Hawaii that was spurned by the Senate, and opened the doors of the American West to thousands of coolie laborers in an 1868 treaty with China. He was forever dickering for naval bases in the Caribbean (though the crumbling American fleet needed new facilities far less than general restoration), but the only deal he could nail down was an agreement to purchase the Danish West Indies (Virgin Islands). The stories of Alaska and the Virgin Islands, in particular, deserve fuller discussion.

The purchase of Alaska accomplished what Seward had always wanted—the extension of American power into the north Pacific—but he fell upon this *coup* as luckily as Jefferson did the Louisiana Purchase. Russia had thought of dumping Alaska for some time because of its economic liabilities and vulnerability to British seizure and had brought the subject up with the United States as early as 1854, and again in 1860. Talks resumed in March 1867 and were concluded in short order with the sale of Alaska to the United States for $7.2 million. As every schoolboy knows, some Americans mocked the new purchase as "Seward's Icebox," but the transaction also received widespread journalistic support (Richard E. Welch, Jr., "American Public Opinion and the Purchase of Russian America," *American Slavic and East European Review*, XVII, December 1958) and quick Senate approval, 37 to 2, after convincing lobbying by Seward on

Alaska's economic and strategic advantages and an erudite supporting speech by Sumner.

Another reason for the Senate's favorable vote was its eagerness not to offend Russia, America's good "friend"—and therein lies a story. Americans had long enjoyed thinking of Russia as a friend, and this sentiment had been confirmed and indeed strengthened in 1863, at the height of the Civil War, when Russian naval fleets paid ostentatiously friendly calls at New York and San Francisco. Excited northerners, still smarting from Europe's hostile attitude to the Union, interpreted the visits as a deliberate show of Russian support for their cause and responded with an emotional outburst of gratitude. A half century after the parades, banquets, and champagne toasts were over, an American scholar discovered that Russia, in fear of an imminent war with Britain, had sent its Baltic and Asiatic fleets to America to prevent their being bottled up by the British in their home ports (F. A. Golder, "The Russian Fleet and the Civil War," *American Historical Review*, XX, July 1915), but Americans high and low, oblivious of this fact, were still awash with the friendship myth in 1867. Only a year earlier, when Czar Alexander II barely escaped an assassination attempt, Congress commended and extended its gratitude to "the nation that had given us its warmest sympathies in our hour of peril." Thomas A. Bailey concludes that the Alaskan treaty "would have failed of ratification" had the Russian ships not made their visit, or had the American people known their real mission ("Why the United States Purchased Alaska," *Pacific Historical Review*, III, February 1934); as it was, a penurious House of Representatives delayed appropriating the purchase price until July 1868, and even then gossip had it that some congressmen's votes may have been bought by the Russian minister.

In 1867, many Americans believed Alaska's main importance was to serve as the northern jaw of a vise relentlessly tightened on British Columbia; the real value of Seward's bargain was not apparent until later on. Meanwhile, Seward's search for Caribbean naval bases continued despite Secretary of the Navy Gideon Welles's lack of enthusiasm for the hunt. Congressional opposition foiled attempts to establish protectorates in Haiti and Santo Domingo or annex part or all of the island of Hispaniola those two republics shared. Success seemed close at hand in 1867 when Seward negotiated the purchase of St. Thomas and St. John in the Danish West Indies, fearing that they might otherwise be sold to Prussia or Austria. A plebiscite in the islands overwhelmingly approved the change and Denmark ratified the instrument in January 1868, but at the last moment Congress balked at the price tag of $7.5 million and raised doubts about the islands' reputation for disaster in light of a hurricane, earthquake, and tidal wave that had struck St. Thomas shortly after the treaty was signed. Efforts to revive the agreement persisted as late as 1870, but to no avail, and it remained for the administration of Woodrow Wilson in 1917 to complete the project Seward had begun.

Seward's imperialism had a buckshot quality to it, but even it seems deliberate by comparison with the expansionism of President Ulysses S. Grant. Most of Grant's expansionist moves, Marilyn B. Young has aptly observed, are best understood "in terms of his total administration, whose dominant characteristic was one of grab." And his grabbiness itself was erratic. He once shrugged off a suggestion to annex French Guiana, apparently from a commendable lack of interest, and he allowed Seward's still-pending Virgin Islands treaty to languish for the simple reason that he did not like Seward. So much for rational motives in foreign policy!

However helter-skelter the course, the Grant administration did continue the trend toward expansionism. In the Pacific, a reciprocal trade agreement of 1875 with Hawaii intimately connected its economy with that of the United States and forbade it to sell any territory to other nations. Three significant moves were made in the Caribbean area. First, Grant's interest in a Central American canal led to a promising treaty with Colombia on transit rights through Panama that the Senate ignored; Grant then appointed a special commission that, shortly before he left office, recommended building a canal through Nicaragua. Second, Grant linked the so-called No Transfer principle to the Monroe Doctrine in 1870 with the statement "that hereafter no territory on this continent shall be regarded as subject to transfer to a European power," a development important in the chronicles of the Monroe Doctrine but of no immediate application.

Grant's third and most significant thrust into the Caribbean was his attempt to annex Santo Domingo. Why did he want Santo Domingo? "Grab" is one answer, glory and power are others. The Dominicans had put it up for sale, and, like President Harding a half century later, Grant always found it hard to say no (Harding's father congratulated his son on his good fortune in not having been born a girl). Among his reasons the President might have listed gaining a naval station, boosting American business, supplying a new home for former slaves, and—in response to the suggestions of a couple of intriguers—making Santo Domingo a sanitarium for future American canal workers afflicted by isthmian fevers. Grant's opportunity for adventure came when the ever impenitent, impecunious, and importunate Dominican rulers once again put their country up for auction. Acting without advice, Grant sent one of his less savory aides, General Orville Babcock, to make a deal. He returned with a treaty that gave the United States, depending on its preference, either full possession of Santo Domingo or the lease of Samana Bay. After renegotiation late in 1869 (Babcock had not been legally authorized to sign a treaty) the wording of the pact called for the purchase of Santo Domingo for $1.5 million or, should that choice not be picked up, the renting of Samaná Bay for $150,000 per annum with a first option to buy.

As the Senate mulled over the treaty, seven American warships patrolled Dominican waters under orders to "destroy or capture" Haitian ships if they attacked the territory. Grant personally cajoled senators in Capitol hallways and made a call at the home of Charles Sumner, leaving with what he thought was a promise of the senator's support. But Sumner attacked the treaty, as did many other Republicans, and in June 1870 it was defeated, ten votes short of ratification. Secretary of State Fish had supported the treaty primarily out of loyalty to Grant and because the president's preoccupation with Santo Domingo gave him a freer hand to deal with the *Alabama* claims and the Cuban Rebellion. The administration tried to resuscitate the project but was unsuccessful, even after purging Sumner from his chairmanship of the Senate Committee on Foreign Relations for his apostasy. Finally, after several attempts at revival, Grant's treaty was given a decent burial.

Senators were not the only opponents of the Santo Domingo scheme. Leading opinion makers throughout the country fought the project, and the arguments they employed directly foreshadowed those of the anti-imperialist movement of 1898–1900. Their attitude, as Ernest R. May has pointed out, coincided with a similar low regard for imperialism that was widely held in Europe in 1870, but the basis of their opposition was uniquely American and rooted in traditional values and current social conditions. The anti-imperialists of the Grant era disliked the cost of expansionist projects, feared the mischief-making potential of an enlarged navy, believed—with the exception of a few genuine liberals on race (like Sumner)—that Reconstruction had already shown the folly of incorporating "alien" races into the American system of government, and also worried about including hundreds of thousands of "semi-savage" Catholics. Most of all, they condemned the Santo Domingo scheme as a dangerous foray into "European" practices repugnant to fundamental American principles (Robert L. Beisner, "Thirty Years Before Manila: E. L. Godkin, Carl Schurz, and Anti-Imperialism in the Gilded Age," *The Historian*, XXX, August 1968).

Another source of anti-imperialist concern was Cuba, where a rebellion that was to last a decade broke out in 1868. By the time Grant took office, the war had become savage, American citizens had been killed, and thousands of dollars' worth of U.S. property had been destroyed. In the United States, Cuban rebel organizations and their American supporters were attracting sympathy and money, and public opinion was beginning to move sharply against Spain.

Americans had taken a special, almost proprietary, interest in Cuba for many years and more than once had intrigued for its cession to the United States. Cuba was the last major European possession near America's southern shores, with an economic potential that tempted American businessmen and a strategic location vis à vis any future isthmian canal. In the early months of the Grant administration, both the president's belligerent tendencies and congressional excitement seemed to presage a course of action that would lead directly to war with Spain and annexation of the island (an idea whispered into the ears of American officials by many Cuban rebels). As a token of Grant's interest, the navy moved ships from the Pacific to the West Indian squadron, enlarging an already sizable flotilla patrolling near Cuban waters.

The greatest obstacle to intervention was Hamilton Fish, who hoped to persuade Spain to end the rebellion through an internal reform of Cuba, thereby avoiding war with Spain and annexation of the turbulent island. He also hoped to keep the Cuban affair from getting in the way of a settlement of the *Alabama* claims. His first task was to prevent Congress from following the example of several Latin American nations in recognizing the rebels' belligerency; such action, he thought, was unjustified by international law and would damage the pending case against Britain's recognition of Confederate belligerency in 1861. It would also make war likely, a development Fish feared on several counts. A war with Spain might not be as easy to win as armchair patriots believed; in any case, it would increase the national debt, complicate and delay solution of serious domestic problems, and lead irresistibly to the annexation of Cuba. A Hudson River aristocrat, Fish sniffed at the pretensions of the Cubans, whom he regarded as totally unsuitable for a place in the American Union. He was convinced that Spain could not suppress the rebellion militarily and repeatedly pressed Madrid to reduce discontent by abolishing slavery and promulgating other social and political reforms.

His success eventually depended on his own dexterity and on domestic and foreign events that fortuitously went his way.

From the start, Fish had to stave off the kind of prorebel feelings embodied in a House resolution of April 9, 1869, that expressed sympathy for the rebellion and empowered Grant to recognize Cuba's independence. Boldly intervening in the summer of 1869, Fish asked Spain to agree to a cease-fire and the abolition of slavery, and to allow the Cubans to purchase their own independence for about $100 million, with the understanding that the United States would guarantee payment. While Spain was hesitating, Grant, without warning, flabbergasted Fish by requesting him to place his official seal on an already prepared proclamation recognizing Cuban belligerency and then issue it. The New Yorker conveniently pigeonholed the document, and Grant, who was by now totally absorbed with things Domini-can, unaccountably forgot all about it! Several months later, in the spring of 1870, Fish staged a showdown. With another belligerency resolution about to emerge from the House cham-ber and with Grant once more rustling about combatively, the secretary of state threatened to resign unless the president ceased interfering in the routine business of his department and publicly dissociated himself from the jingoes by demanding that the House squelch its pending resolution. The victor of Appo-mattox retreated. Fish for the first time took unchallenged control of Cuban policy, and the House—having received Grant's message—defeated the offending resolution on June 16, 1870, by a vote of 101 to 88.

Thereafter, the Cuban problem remained quiet until 1873 when an unpredictable new turn threatened to torpedo Fish's well-laid plans. In October, the *Virginius*, a rebel-owned vessel laden with arms and fraudulently flying the Stars and Stripes, was seized by a Spanish warship in international waters and taken to a Cuban port where fifty-three of its passengers and crew, including some U.S. citizens, were executed by a firing squad after kangaroo-court trials. Fish could hardly contain the initial uproar at home, but when it became known that the ship's American registry was fraudulent, passions subsided and Spain (glad to get off so easily) agreed to pay an $80,000 indemnity to the families of U.S. citizens from the *Virginius* who had been executed.

In 1875 Fish made one more attempt, unsuccessful as it turned out, to end the Cuban civil war, but the likelihood of a Spanish–U.S. conflict decreased rapidly after the climactic events of 1873.

A comparison of the peaceful resolution of the *Virginius* affair and the war crisis of 1898 is worthwhile at this point. There are six important differences between the two cases. (1) War was far less acceptable in the autumn of deep depression of 1873 than it was in the prosperous spring of 1898. (2) In 1873 many Americans were sympathetic to the Spanish government, then under brief republican rule, while in 1898 no such reason for sympathy existed. (3) Few Americans doubted the fraudulent status of the *Virginius*, but in 1898 most were certain the *Maine* had been the innocent victim of foul play. (4) Spain seemed eager to make amends in 1873 but stubbornly intransigent twenty-five years later. (5) U.S. public opinion, capable of being aroused by foreign alarms only fitfully in the 1870s, was thoroughly jingoistic by 1898. (6) The man in charge of the crisis in 1873 was adamantly opposed to war while those in power in 1898 were expansion-minded and in some cases downright eager for armed conflict. (For details one must still go to Allan Nevins, *Hamilton Fish: The Inner History of the Grant Administration* [1936]; a briefer outline agreeing on most points is in Lester D. Langley, *The Cuban Policy of the United States: A Brief History* [1968]; sinister imperialist designs are detected in Fish's conduct by Philip Foner in *A History of Cuba and Its Relations with the United States*, vol. II [1963].)

The civil war in Cuba ended in 1878, and slavery was soon abolished, but Spain's continued harsh rule guaranteed another round of violence. In the meantime, American economic influence in the island increased significantly. Even during the war years of 1868–78, the volume of U.S. trade with Cuba reached a higher level than with all other Latin American nations combined; profiting from wartime disruptions, American investors had succeeded in replacing many Cubans and Spaniards as landowners. Fish had kept the United States out of the war and indirectly aided American penetration of the Cuban economy. In his intermittent support of Cuban independence, he had also moved away from John Quincy Adams's policy of tolerating Spanish rule until the time was ripe for a U.S. takeover, and had departed as well from the push for immediate annexation that had characterized the 1840s and 1850s. But his achievement should not be exaggerated; the United States did not have so much a Cuban "policy" as a Fish policy, which could be altered 180 degrees in a twinkling. Real continuity in Cuban policy was not to appear until the emergence in the nineties of the New Paradigm.

James G. Blaine's nine months as secretary of state in 1881 furnish the third example of allegedly systematic, expansionist policymaking in the era of the Old Paradigm. This characterization is based on his invitation to eighteen Western Hemisphere republics to attend an inter-American conference in Washington. Though the conference was canceled after his resignation late in 1881 (to be revived and, in fact, chaired by Blaine in 1889–90 during his second tour at the State Department), his role in laying the cornerstone of Pan-Americanism has been frequently interpreted as a farsighted attempt to promote peaceful settlement of hemispheric disputes and, in the view of markets-minded historians, to create the means for capturing the export markets of Latin America.

Blaine was probably more worried about European political influence in the hemisphere than export markets, but the poor trading record of the United States in the area and the many local wars did concern him. The two issues were closely connected. Maintaining hemispheric peace would encourage trade generally, closer U.S. ties with Latin America would help promote the sale of American products, and peace and increased U.S. exports would, in turn, reduce European influence in the area. Thus described, Blaine's reasoning seems impressively logical, but a more likely explanation of his 1881 Pan-Americanism suggests itself. Blaine took office with no previous experience in foreign affairs and had never before mentioned the conference idea, but he was known as an inveterate activist who hoped to be not only President Garfield's "prime minister," but his successor as well. It was to his direct political advantage to conduct what came to be called a "spirited" foreign policy. Ready at hand was a set of tempting inter-American issues, the perfect arena for a display of "spirit," and Blaine plunged in—with alarming results.

First he dived into a boundary dispute betwen Mexico and Guatemala, asking Mexico to accept impartial arbitration while making his own partiality for Guatemala all too apparent. Mexico initially was polite in its demurral but, when Blaine persisted, testily rejected his proposal. The dispute dragged on in spite of Blaine, whose only accomplishment had been to offend neighboring Mexico. Farther south, where Costa Rica and Colombia had recently agreed to have a European nation arbitrate a similar border argument, Blaine—suspicious of European intrusions—chimed in with loud but futile protests and again netted only a lowering of U.S. stock in Latin America. His third such intervention ensnared him in the War of the Pacific, which since 1879 had pitted Chile against Peru and Bolivia in a struggle for control of coastal areas rich in nitrates and guano. Chile had won the military contest handily but could not wrap up the peace because her opponents refused to accept her retention of large territorial gains. The United States had tried once before to mediate the impasse without success, but Blaine was eager to try again, partly for the political gains that might accrue at home and partly to take a stand against armed expansion, cut pro-British Chile down to size, and aid the Peruvians to keep them from seeking help in Europe. In sum, it added up to another partisan intervention that would get nowhere. Chile bristled in anger. America's reputation suffered from the spectacle of the U.S. minister in Santiago taking Chile's side, his colleague in Lima taking Peru's side, and the two attacking each other in public; as one historian has said, Blaine's ministers were "ill-paid, ill-trained, and ill-tempered."

Belatedly aware of the difficulties accompanying the role of mediator, Blaine sought desperately to rescue his "spirited" foreign policy. He sent a special agent to South America to reestablish a unified American position on the War of the Pacific and line up support for it from Brazil and Argentina and then persuaded the new president, Chester A. Arthur, to issue formal invitations for an inter-American conference. According to Russell H. Bastert, whose argument is supported by impressive evidence, Blaine had three goals in mind: to recoup his political fortunes, restore at least the appearance of success to the shambles of his Latin American policy by means of a grand gesture, and use the presence of other states at his inter-American conference to force Mexico and Chile into line on the two pending issues. While in office Blaine had never mentioned commercial expansion as an important objective of the conference; that theme appeared only after he left office and responded to attacks made on his record as secretary of state ("Diplomatic Reversal: Frelinghuysen's Opposition to Blaine's Pan-American Policy in 1882," *Mississippi Valley Historical Review*, XLII, March 1956; "A New Approach to Blaine's Pan-American Policy," *Hispanic American Historical Review*, XXXIX, August 1959). Of course, Blaine's manifold problems stemmed in part from his ambitious conception of United States diplomatic interests; nonetheless, his 1881 "expansionism" must in the end be characterized as a hodgepodge of hasty patch jobs, political opportunism, and misdirected energy.

Blaine's successor, Frederick T. Frelinghuysen, certainly had no thought of damaging an important "policy" when he withdrew the conference invitations. On the contrary, he had evidence that both Chile and Mexico, as well as the governments of several European nations, were deeply suspicious of the scheduled gathering and that a few individuals close to Blaine stood to profit financially from an anti-Chilean settlement of the War of the Pacific. Eventually the United States did help bring this war to an end, though not the underlying conflicts that had caused it, but she reaped no goodwill for her efforts. Few mediators ever have.

DAY-TO-DAY DIPLOMATIC
PREOCCUPATIONS

Unquestionably Seward, Grant, and Blaine all took America some distance down the road to imperialism, but not with consistency of purpose and not because the journey seemed essential. They veered with the wind, acting more like impulsive jingoes than policy-minded diplomatists. They showed less concern for the national interests of the United States than for their own political careers. In these ways they were quintessentially men of the Old Paradigm. It is important to recall once more that the day-to-day preoccupations of American diplomatic officials in the 1870s and 1880s usually concerned the kind of trivial and routine matter almost never reported by historians (Milton Plesur's *America's Outward Thrust* is a welcome exception). For example, they spent much energy protecting American citizens (many of them naturalized) who got into difficulties abroad: Irish-Americans meddling in the movement for a free Ireland, Jews harassed while visiting Russia or making pilgrimages to Palestine, and—the most trouble-prone of all—Christian missionaries, whose faraway imbroglios account for innumerable boxes of records in the National Archives. Another example of such time-consuming but uncelebrated issues was the constant friction with Mexico caused by horse thieves and border bandits, which led in the seventies and eighties to nearly twenty retaliatory border crossings by U.S. troopers. In time these fracases along the Rio Grande gave way to a more momentous border traffic—Americans headed south to invest money in Mexican mines, railroads, and petroleum—but while they lasted, the petty raids and counterraids monopolized the time of many an American official in both Washington and Mexico City.

Most of the important issues that faced American policymakers in this period arose within the Western Hemisphere. The one that came to galvanize attention on hemispheric affairs was that hardy perennial, the interoceanic canal. In the wake of several U.S. failures in the 1860s and 1870s to gain a canal site by treaty, the announcement in 1879 that a French company headed by Ferdinand de Lesseps of Suez Canal fame would begin work on a canal through Panama seemed particularly threatening to statesmen in Washington. The Senate and House each passed a condemnatory resolution, and President Hayes declared on March 8, 1880, that the United States could not tolerate a canal controlled by "any European power [de Lesseps, however, represented a private firm, not the French government] or . . . combination of European powers," and added for good measure that a canal "would be . . . virtually a part of the coast line of the United States." De Lesseps, whose company went bankrupt in ten years, was only one problem for the United States. Another was how to undo the Clayton-Bulwer Treaty, which had been signed in 1850 and forbade the building or operation of a canal except as a joint enterprise with Great Britain. Attempts to untie this obnoxious knot climaxed in the remarkable Nicaraguan treaty of 1884, in which the United States finally gained its route across Central America, but only by pretending that the 1850 treaty with Britain had never existed. The Senate, squirming at this blatant pretext and leery of provisions that committed the United States to protect Nicaraguan sovereignty, sighed with regret and voted to defeat the agreement. A motion to reconsider gave new hope to treaty supporters, but President Cleveland permanently withdrew the treaty from the Senate shortly after his inauguration in 1885, and there the matter stood for another fifteen years.

A constant problem for the United States was Canada, a nation once described by Samuel F. Bemis as the "coupling-pin" of U.S.–British relations and the source of almost every point of conflict still outstanding between Washington and London. Many sources of friction appeared in the latter part of the nineteenth century, including the Fenians' raids across the Canadian border in the 1860s, which were calculated to help Ireland by causing trouble between Britain and America, but the most vexatious was the issue of American rights in Canadian fishing grounds. Questions of cod had so relentlessly plagued U.S.–British relations that one might suppose that the Founding

Fathers of 1787 had concluded their constitutional labors with a special injunction stating: "It shall be the duty of the Executive, Congress and People alike to argue in perpetuity with Great Britain over the fisheries of His Britannic Majesty's Dominions of North America." The argument had started even before 1787 but was supposedly settled by the Treaty of Washington in 1871. In subsequent years, however, this settlement broke down, was patched up, and then collapsed again in 1886. Canada began seizing and fining American violators. Congress retaliated by empowering the president to keep all Canadian goods and ships out of American waters, but Cleveland used these powers only as a "bargaining chip" and secured a new agreement in 1888, only to have it rejected by a partisan Republican Senate. While he and Congress continued to wrangle to no purpose, practical diplomats worked out a two-year *modus vivendi* that, renewed periodically, remained the basis for regulation of the Canadian fisheries until 1898–99 when another attempt, equally futile, was made to settle the matter permanently.

A different kind of dispute broke out in the Bering Sea in 1886 when the United States cracked down on Canadians engaged in pelagic sealing—the hunting of seals at sea rather than on their island homes. In Professor Bemis's classic description: "Amphibious is the fur seal, ubiquitous and carnivorous, uniparous, gregarious and withal polygamous." Their home was an American possession, the Pribilof Islands, where thousands were killed annually, but under restrictions designed to preserve the herd. Pelagic sealing, which did not limit the number of kills and led to the killing of many females, threatened the herd's existence and interfered with an important American commercial enterprise. American seizures of Canadian ships on the high seas in 1886–87 provoked angry protests from Ottawa and London, whereupon Congress proclaimed the waters in question a closed sea (*mare clausum*) under domestic American jurisdiction, and new seizures began in 1889. A severe crisis seemed imminent when Britain threatened to use naval force to protect Canadian sealers. C. S. Campbell, Jr. has demonstrated in "The Anglo-American Crisis in the Bering Sea, 1890–1891" (*Missis-*

sippi Valley Historical Review, XLVIII, December 1961) that the diplomatic logjam began to break after it was revealed that American sealing practices were as dangerous to the seal herd as pelagic sealing. A temporary *modus vivendi* was worked out in 1891, and in the following year it was agreed to submit the question to international arbitration. The arbitrators, meeting in Paris in 1893, ruled flatly against the United States on the *mare clausum* question, ordered it to pay damages to the Canadians, and restricted future U.S. rights to the traditional three-mile limit from the shores of the seal islands. But they also took measures to protect the herd by designating a zone within sixty miles of the islands closed to all seal fishing and forbidding all pelagic sealing for three months of each year. Another dispute with Canada was thus settled, and the trend toward better U.S.–British relations continued despite Fenians, fish, and fur seals. (An excellent account of the denouement is Campbell's "The Bering Sea Settlements of 1892," *Pacific Historical Review*, XXXII, November 1963; the Anglo-Canadian side of the story is in Robert C. Brown, *Canada's National Policy, 1883–1900: A Study in Canadian-American Relations* [1964].)

U.S. involvement in Europe remained minimal. One of the few issues that disturbed the calm of America's ties to the Continent arose in the 1880s when both France and Germany placed severe restrictions on the importation of American meat products, especially pork. Their official justifications emphasized the questionable condition of the meat and were at least partially legitimate, but what was probably at the bottom of the "pork disputes" was an effort to protect French and German livestock growers from American competition. The problem was solved in 1890–91, but not until the United States had threatened to retaliate by cutting off all imports from countries discriminating against American products and had also threatened to impose severe restrictions on the sale of German sugar in the United States. In southern and eastern Europe, Big Power diplomacy concentrated increasingly on the tottering Ottoman Empire. The result was a reduction in the modest American presence established earlier in such places as Greece, Turkey,

Bulgaria, and Egypt by a few missionaries, merchants, educators, naval officers, and an occasional diplomat. These Americans had merely been dabbling in an area about which the Russians and British were deadly serious. When Washington officials discovered, during the Bulgarian massacres of the 1870s, that some Americans were playing with dynamite, they abruptly put an end to it.

America's chronic lack of interest in Africa underwent little change, even after Captain Robert Shufeldt in the late 1870s gained U.S. rights to a coaling station in Madagascar, signed a commercial treaty with the Sultan of Johanna in the Comoro Islands, visited Zanzibar and the Persian Gulf, and urged his government to encourage trade along the western coast of Africa. There were murmurs of approval in Washington in response to the plea for trade, but quite predictably no specific action followed. Another illustration of the sputtering nature of American expansionism appeared when Grover Cleveland reversed an African initiative, unusual in itself, of the Arthur administration. Arthur, having previously requested international cooperation in establishing a commercial open door in the Congo—an area of intense European competition—agreed to send delegates to the Berlin Conference on the Congo in 1884. His delegation signed the Berlin Treaty and did much to insure the inclusion of provisions for free commerce and river navigation. Arthur approved their work but was soon out of office. The incoming Cleveland, who specialized in burying the pending handiwork of his predecessors, refused to submit the document, in his opinion dangerously entangling, to the Senate.

In Asia and the Pacific, the United States pursued an assertive and even adventurous policy in the 1865–89 period that resulted in markedly increased activity in China, Japan, Korea, Samoa, and Hawaii. Yet this intensified involvement took place comfortably within the perimeters of the Old Paradigm: it was erratic, cautious, frequently amateurish, and almost never initiated in Washington; few officials, either at home or abroad, saw the new boldness in the Pacific and Asia as being essential to American interests.

In China, the United States generally continued its "jackal diplomacy," picking up change from the sidewalk after European thugs had rolled the Chinaman for his wad of bills. She cooperated in punitive expeditions organized by Britain and France to enforce the "unequal-treaty" system that obliged China to grant many concessions damaging to Chinese pride and sovereignty and took advantage of her own status as a "most-favored nation" to receive automatically any commercial concession granted to other nations. Through these means the United States joined the European powers in enjoying open ports, low tariffs, and extraterritorial rights in China. A potent myth was growing in the United States that America was deeply appreciated by the Chinese for her allegedly unique generosity among Western powers, but most members of the American community in China neither adored the Chinese nor had any illusions about China's view of the United States. In 1883 one of the ablest Americans ever to serve as minister to China, John Russell Young, lashed out at the Imperial Court's "eunuchs, . . . pink buttoned censors who read the stars . . . and all that mass of thieving treacherous, cowardly cunning adventurers which surround the throne and live an insectiverous, parasitic existence on this venerable and august monarchy." At home most Americans who met honest-to-goodness Chinese disliked them, and no sooner had large numbers of coolies begun entering the United States after the Burlingame Treaty of 1868 than a popular cry arose to stop the flow. A new treaty of 1880 obliged the United States to provide ample protection to Chinese already in the country but permitted it to "regulate, limit, or suspend" the entry of additional Chinese workers in a "reasonable" way. Congress's response in 1882 was to "suspend" Chinese immigration for a "reasonable" period of twenty years, amended to ten years after President Arthur vetoed the more extreme measure. In 1888 Congress imposed a total ban on Chinese immigration following lynchings of Chinese in Wyoming and Washington Territory, even though this action represented a unilateral abrogation of the 1880 treaty.

American influence in Japan declined following the Civil

War because no one cared sufficiently to exploit Commodore Matthew Perry's historic opening of the nation in 1854. The only noteworthy development until late in the 1890s was Washington's decision to break with other white nations and support "treaty revision" that would involve surrendering some extraterritorial rights and turning back to Japan more control over her port regulations and tariff rates. After several false starts, these changes were embodied in a pact negotiated in 1894. Though America's voluntary renunciation of special rights resulted, not surprisingly, in a further reduction of her influence in Japan, American statesmen either failed to notice the fact or considered it unimportant.

In the meantime the United States was inaugurating relations with nearby Korea. Understanding the "Hermit Kingdom's" relationship to China, which claimed suzerainty over Korea but no responsibility for her actions, was beyond the power of most American minds. A U.S. naval squadron had unsuccessfully attempted to open Korea to outside influence in 1871, but eleven years later the prospects looked better. China was now interested in using an outside power as a counterweight to Japan, which in 1876 had pried Korea open *à la* Perry. The same Captain Shufeldt who had earlier made a diplomatically significant voyage to Africa arrived in China on the *Ticonderoga* in 1881, proceeded to hold months of talks on Korea with Chinese officials, and finally completed in 1882 a treaty that he then took to Seoul for official Korean signature. It covered standard commercial issues and permitted the opening of an official diplomatic mission in Korea. What was remarkable about the Shufeldt treaty, however, was the Old Paradigm manner in which it was negotiated and its immediate consequences. Shufeldt had only the most casual instructions from Secretary of State Blaine; when he cabled home for additional guidance at a crucial moment in the discussions, he received no reply at all, not even the courtesy of an acknowledgement. Furthermore, neither he nor the State Department fully realized the significance of his refusal to accept a provision that would have explicitly acknowledged Korean dependence on China, the absence of which weakened China in her contest with Japan for Korean supremacy. In spite of itself, the United States probably wielded more influence in Seoul in 1883 and 1884 than any other foreign power, only to retreat to the sidelines and watch Japan, China, and Russia jostle for position. As in Japan, America had forfeited the foothold previously gained. Few at home cared.

Many cared, however, about Hawaii and Samoa. President John Tyler had declared as early as 1842 that the United States would not tolerate a European takeover of Hawaii, an important intermediate point in the China trade, port for American whalers, and field of missionary activity. After several inconclusive gestures toward annexation in the 1850s and early 1870s, America's grip began to tighten. This was apparent in the reciprocal trade treaty of 1875 mentioned previously, which allowed Hawaiian sugar into the United States duty-free and consequently stimulated Hawaiian sugar-growing and closely tied the islands into the American economy. Hawaii also promised in 1875 not to sell any of its territory to other nations. The grip intensified upon renewal of the treaty in 1887, especially when a provision added at the Senate's insistence granted the use and control of Pearl Harbor to the United States. In 1887 Washington rejected an Anglo-French proposal for a three-way guarantee of Hawaii's independence and neutrality; eventual U.S. annexation now seemed inevitable, but the actual turn of events that brought the islands fully into the American embrace is a tale that belongs to the 1890s and the New Paradigm.

It is less apparent why Americans became so excited about faraway Samoa in the South Pacific, but the fact remains that these islands inspired an uncharacteristically forward-looking policy. The first Americans on the scene were a shady group of land speculators and petty merchants, but before long official U.S. attention was attracted to the excellent harbor of Pago Pago, badly wanted by the navy. The details of what happened from 1872, when the Senate rejected a treaty granting possession of Pago Pago to the United States, until 1899, when the United States and Germany partitioned the islands between themselves, would interest only a few specialists—or devotees of comic opera. With such Americans as Albert B. Steinberger and Berthild Greenebaum in starring roles amid a predominantly German cast and with Robert Louis Stevenson fortuitously on hand to write the libretto (*A Footnote to History: Eight Years of Trouble in Samoa* [1892]), the show lasted nearly three decades, each act ending with a new Samoan chief saluting the freshly raised flag of either Germany, America, or England, the symbolic gesture soon to be disavowed by the respective home government. The climactic scene was the great storm of 1889 which, as one would expect in such a script, arrived just in time to batter to pieces the German and American warships that were about to exchange hostile fire. Along the way the United States took over Pago Pago in 1878, joined Britain and Germany in a tripartite Samoan condominium in 1889, and formally divided the islands with Germany in 1899 after the British dropped out. Samoa never had the naval significance anticipated for it, but the years of intrigue and conflict that went into its acquisition contributed in no small measure to the rise of an expansionist spirit in the United States. (The standard treatment is Sylvia Masterman, *The Origins of International Rivalry in Samoa, 1845–1884* [1934]; a newer account more concerned with the Samoans themselves, R. P. Gilson, *Samoa 1830 to 1900: The Politics of a Multi-Cultural Community* [1970], adds little to the story line but contains many interesting interpretative commentaries.)

Why that spirit became so strong in the nineties and how it helped to transform American foreign policy into a far more serious business remain to be discussed.

THREE

From the Old to the New Foreign Policy Paradigm

SUDDEN BLOWS TO THE OLD PARADIGM

A new era in American diplomatic history opened sometime around 1890, and the policymaker of 1895 differed sharply from his 1885 predecessor. The Old diplomatic Paradigm gave way to the New. But what caused this change? What were the characteristics of the New Paradigm? What remnants of the old epoch persisted into the new?

A paradigm change is related to changes in both conditions and the perception of those conditions. Over a long enough period of time circumstances themselves usually change sufficiently to make an old paradigm obsolete. A foreign policy conceived in the days of rickety biplanes, for example, will not work in an age of intercontinental ballistic missiles. When the givens of the past need to be reexamined, they lose their status as givens, making way for new ones to come along. The same thing can happen even when "objective" circumstances change very little if people begin to look at them from a significantly different perspective. It can be argued, for instance, that the only major change that occurred in the Cuban situation from the 1870s to the 1890s was the way in which Americans looked at it. Hamilton Fish's generation, though not unsympathetic to the Cuban rebels of their day, was prepared to stand by and do nothing while Spain suppressed the rebellion; William McKinley's generation was unwilling to remain passive in almost identical circumstances. In most cases, however, altered circumstances *and* outlook combine to produce a shift in paradigms. Certainly this was true in the replacement of the Old by the New Paradigm.

Unlike the scientific paradigms discussed by Thomas S. Kuhn, diplomatic paradigms are unlikely to change overnight. But the Old Paradigm did fall quite abruptly, suggesting that in addition to the inevitable erosion from factors working gradually over a period of time, it sustained severe shocks that accelerated the process dramatically. Of these sudden blows, three closely related ones deserve attention in an analysis of the paradigm shift that inaugurated the American diplomatic "revolution" of the nineties. Two occurred at home, and one abroad. The first was a general social malaise that plunged many Americans into a state of gloom and anxiety in the late eighties and early nineties; the second was a severe economic depression in the mid-nineties that exacerbated the malaise; and the third was an apparent and unlooked-for threat to U.S. export markets in Europe and China that was especially upsetting in light of the two preceding blows.

The Social Malaise. A social malaise can be defined as a widespread feeling of uneasiness among people, a confusion about the present and anxiety about the future. This phenomenon has been imaginatively treated in the late Richard Hofstadter's analysis of what he called the "psychic crisis" of the nineties ("Cuba, the Philippines, and Manifest Destiny," in *The Paranoid Style in American Politics and Other Essays* [1965]; the original version of this essay appeared in 1952). The essence of this crisis was a sudden shaking of confidence in the viability of American institutions, a suspicion that the quality of the American population was deteriorating, and a chilling awareness that America, normally considered on a preordained course toward bigger and better things, was unpredictably adrift, feelings especially experienced by intellectuals and other opinion makers.

Several tangible developments led to this intangible sense of unease. One was the change taking place in U.S. demography. The rapid growth of population from 39 million in 1870 to 63 million in 1890 was unsettling enough (a comparable rise from 1950 to 1970 would have been from 151 to 244 million, instead of the actual 203 million). Growth alone was less disturbing than the makeup of that growth; 520,000 immigrants, on an average, arrived annually during the 1880s. Many Americans were concerned that the high volume of immigration would pose a threat to social homogeneity and unity, especially in light of the dramatic shift during the nineties in the sources of immigration from northern and western to southern and eastern Europe. The new people seemed unusually alien to "natives" for a variety of understandable reasons. As Russian Jews, Italians, Greeks, and Ruthenians poured into the country (instead of more assimilable Germans and Norwegians), the feeling grew among native Americans that the foundation of their society was shifting under them.

Another development of the eighties and nineties that made the time seem out of joint was the extraordinary growth of

American cities, ill equipped and poorly organized for the new demands placed upon them, but nonetheless home to millions of immigrants and uprooted farmers and villagers. Watching the urban problems multiply and the American countryside empty out, many Americans were reminded of Thomas Jefferson's prediction of social disaster if a yeoman society should ever be supplanted by hordes of city-dwellers.

An additional blow to American tranquillity was the rapid consolidation of domestic business firms into giant "trusts" and the less effective but equally unfamiliar rise of labor unions in numbers, membership, and militancy. Middle-class entrepreneurs, rising professional men, and old-style artisans all felt ground between the top and bottom stones of organized economic power, and the feeling grew that opportunities for the individual, the common man, were declining rapidly. In a land of individual opportunity, this was no small thing. Why was there a "Sugar Trust" when every man was supposed to have a chance for a piece of the pie? Why was the Senate said to be a club of millionaires in a country where Abe Lincoln was able to become president?

Worse still, the mid-nineties brought what seemed to many Americans a new parade of horrors: the crushing panic and depression of 1893–97, the unsettling discovery that class conflict had dared to show its scarred face in the United States, and an explosion of radicalism and large-scale social conflicts— Populism, the Homestead Strike, the Pullman Boycott, Coxey's March on Washington, Bryan's free-silver campaign, the rise of Eugene Debs, and an indigenous socialist party. Amid such turmoil, it was not uncommon to hear Americans speak fearfully of a new Jacobin Revolution or the fall of a latter-day Rome.

A notable attempt to explain some of these changes in American life was made by the young historian Frederick Jackson Turner, who in 1893 proclaimed the end of an epoch with the supposed disappearance of the American frontier. He credited the frontier experience with having produced America's national character, democratic government, and, by implication, her economic prosperity, and those who heard his thesis found the thought of a frontierless future unpromising indeed. Other writers soon popularized Turner's frontier message, especially its contemporary overtones, and before long a public speaker was judged remiss if he neglected to comment on the problems of a society that no longer possessed a frontier safety valve. Time and again, pundits warned that the United States was in for declining opportunities and mushrooming social crises unless it could find some substitute for the frontier to generate growth and progress. This line of reasoning led invariably to the conclusion, which Turner himself had barely intimated, that the United States must find a new frontier to absorb its dynamic energies and supply a new foundation for its traditional way of life—a frontier of export markets and colonies.

As Richard Hofstadter suggests, one important consequence of these waves of doubt and frustration about America's continued strength and purpose was a burst of aggressive energy aimed at restoring those qualities. Some of this energy went into campaigns for social and political reform at home, but much of it sought expression in an expansionist foreign policy. Perhaps the United States could reaffirm its soundness by thrashing some other country in a war or, more subtly, by demonstrating its ability to govern "inferior" peoples in a colonial empire. Once indifferent to events outside their boundaries, Americans now searched abroad for the means to internal salvation.

Seen in a broader context, the social malaise of the late eighties and early nineties produced a grudging opening of American minds to new and previously unacceptable ideas because the old ones had failed them. In a period of drastic social change, old maxims lost their sway over people who had good reason to take them for granted no longer; calm and thoughtful Americans, as well as frightened and anxious ones, felt compelled by events to reexamine the precepts of U.S. foreign policy. Perhaps Washington's and Jefferson's warnings against foreign entanglements were wrong, or inapplicable to modern times; perhaps the traditional taboo against colonialism now stood in the way of American progress and even of basic national safety. Accepted givens were no longer "given."

The Panic and Depression. Although much in evidence by 1893, America's malaise intensified and drew more people into its gloomy embrace during the shattering depression that struck in that year. The depression did more than undermine American optimism; as Walter LaFeber has pointed out, it caused unprecedented interest in foreign trade as a solution to the crisis. Arriving just as the United States was about to outstrip Great Britain as the world's leading industrial nation and manufactured exports were beginning to overtake agricultural and raw-material exports in dollar value, the depression seemed to demonstrate cruelly and urgently the economic and social need for a massive increase in exports to foreign markets. This proposition, whether actually "true" or not, was accepted as true in the 1890s by businessmen, politicians, and publicists alike. An always vigorous interest in foreign trade now took on obsessive proportions. The matter could no longer be handled through the traditionally casual methods of promotion but now demanded continuous and systematic attention at the highest levels of the state.

The Threat to Old Markets. The export problem seemed urgent by the mid-nineties; a few years later it seemed almost desperate because of rising tariffs in Europe and European colonies and the sudden descent of Japan and the great powers of Europe on China in such a whirlwind of leaseholds, spheres of influence, and annexations that the total disappearance of the ancient Empire seemed likely. How was the United States to survive the emergency of the nineties if, in addition to needing new markets for its economic surplus, its already established markets suddenly collapsed as a result of Britain's recent move toward protectionism, the sudden rise of tariff walls against American products throughout continental Europe, and the parceling-out of China? It was widely believed that the United States must either take decisive diplomatic action or suffer potential economic disaster.

THE IMPACT
OF CUMULATIVE CHANGE

Thus a series of abrupt dislocations contributed substantially to a reexamination of old diplomatic axioms. Where there had been social stability, economic progress, and open foreign markets, there were now rocking social foundations, a catastrophic depression, and iron shutters rolled down around the world against American tradesmen. Although these sudden and unforeseen developments were necessary to the fall of the Old Paradigm, they were not sufficient to the task. Other factors—slow-working and cumulative—did much in undermining the old patterns.

National Growth and Progress. The thirty years that passed after the Civil War inevitably left their mark on U.S. foreign policy. American economic growth, for instance, not only produced the troublesome surplus we have already noted but also greatly augmented American influence in international affairs. The increased awareness among Americans of their country's growing wealth and numbers spurred change as well. As Senator Orville H. Platt of Connecticut told a reporter in 1893: "A policy of isolation did well enough when we were an embryo nation, but today things are different. . . . We are sixty-five million of people, the most advanced and powerful on earth, and regard to our future welfare demands an abandonment of the doctrines of isolation."

Technological advances also had their effect. Progress in transportation and communication meant that the outer world was more accessible than ever before, an alluring thought to imaginative men, but also that distant events were more likely to impinge on the interests of the United States, a fact that called for a more security-minded diplomacy. In addition, technological improvements in the art of war made the United States more vulnerable to attack and stimulated interest among some Americans—especially those concerned with the navy—in sharing the benefits of martial technology.

A New Generation. Another factor that probably influenced the paradigm change was the fading away of a
generation whose central life experience had been the Civil War.
Although the war spawned a lot of old-campground nostalgia,
the men of both sides who had fought it were, for the most part,
cool to further military adventure and sacrifice in their lifetime.
They were intimately familiar with the terrible and inglorious
realities of war and knew the ruin it had caused in the lives of
many of them and the disappointing legacy of political and
racial problems it had left. As a Boston publisher who had been
wounded in the Civil War wrote during the Venezuela crisis: "I
have . . . seen enough of war and its effects to induce me to use
every effort in my power to prevent the spread of any desire for
war with any country." Their tithe of strife and self-sacrifice
paid, they threw themselves with relief into America's favorite
new activity of moneymaking. By the early nineties, however,
new men were rising to power and influence, a generation
somewhat skeptical of commercial values, without the memories
of a stirring moral crusade, and with no war—the meaning of
which they divined only from idealized reminiscences and
romantic magazine engravings—to call their own.

Nationalism. Just as gradually changing circumstances
helped to set the stage for important diplomatic change, so did
shifting currents of ideas and attitudes. Imperial powers are
rarely deficient in *amour-propre*, and few periods of American
history were as blatantly nationalistic as the 1890s. Patriotic
societies and historical associations sprang up on all sides, an
"Americanization" movement initiated immigrants into the
glories and customs of their adopted nation, and the public
schools increasingly dedicated themselves to instilling patriotism
in their young charges. Some sophisticates were not pleased, like
the editorial writer of the New York *Journal of Commerce* who
complained in 1895 that: "This rage of displaying the flag in
season and out of season, this remarkable fashion of hanging the
flag over every schoolhouse and of giving boys military drill, and
this passion for tracing one's ancestry to somebody who fought
in the Revolutionary War or the War of 1812, or at least against

the French and Indians, all help to create a false spirit of militarism." In three years' time the militarism would become real.

Expansionist Thought. Surges of extravagant nationalism had appeared before in the nation's history, as in the 1820s, without being channeled into imperialism. What distinguished the popular nationalism of the nineties was the wave of expansionist thought, both implicit and explicit, that accompanied it. The imperialist tendencies of some thinkers normally associated with the rise of American expansionism—such as Alfred T. Mahan, the naval strategist; Brooks Adams, the geopolitician and philosopher; and Josiah Strong, the ardent missionary—have perhaps been exaggerated (see, for example, Dorothea R. Muller, "Josiah Strong and American Nationalism: A Reevaluation," *Journal of American History*, LIII, December 1966), but the paths they charted led unquestionably toward imperialism. Probably the most important of these thinkers was Mahan, whose *The Influence of Seapower upon History* was published in 1890. Mahan directed his main assault against the traditional American emphasis on coastal defense and commerce-raiding, insisting that a great power must have a navy that could carry the battle directly to the enemy's fleet. Purely naval arguments were not his only concern, however. Sharing the contemporary obsession with foreign markets and believing that America's energies and talents justified her attempt to dominate less "vital" and productive peoples, Mahan sketched out a program based on increasing exports, acquiring a few colonies to supply American industry with raw materials and consume its finished products, building a large, swift navy to protect America's overseas possessions and shipping lanes, and constructing an isthmian canal and obtaining a few coaling and repair bases, especially in the Pacific and East Asia, to support the navy. Many Americans found the formula irresistible.

In the boiled-down and popularized versions that reached the public, Social Darwinism also became a staple of expansionist thought. It was important for two reasons. First, by positing struggle and contention as the roots of progress and even survival, this evolutionary theory suggested that an exclusive preoccupation with peace and prosperity would eventually make the United States soft and weak, an easy prey for hardier and more disciplined peoples. Second, Darwinism gave "scientific" sanction to racism and buttressed the idea that the world was truly composed, as white Americans had long liked to think, of greater and lesser breeds. The inability of Asian, African, and, for that matter, Latin American peoples to deny the will of great powers merely demonstrated their unfitness in the life struggle. Imposing colonial rule over such peoples seemed, therefore, more an act of benevolence than a regrettable violation of American principles. This rationale was growing in popularity at the very time many northerners were concluding that the freed slaves had failed the test of freedom offered them after the Civil War and would have to be returned, at least temporarily, to the safekeeping of southern whites. Disillusion with Reconstruction and the philosophy of Social Darwinism reinforced each other perfectly.

Closely related to Social Darwinism was the doctrine of "Anglo-Saxonism," which also prepared American minds for imperialism. It taught that the Anglo-Saxons were highest of all on the evolutionary ladder; one of their many points of superiority was a rare skill in the art of government, which uniquely qualified them for an imperial role. It is puzzling that this idea arose during one of the more uninspired eras of American politics—it may, of course, have provided a timely reassurance—but, in any case, Anglo-Saxonism further justified expansionist policies and also gave Americans reason to believe that they were more suited for imperial power than other undeniably "fit" nations like Germany and Russia.

Missionaries. American missionaries did much to arouse expansionist sentiment. A Methodist clergyman returning from a 1900 visit to Puerto Rico was convinced that religious services "in neat, attractive churches, with plenty of good singing . . . with Sunday school, young people's societies, etc., each church becoming a social center, would command many worshipers." The desire to carry God's Message to the heathen (quite often, more accurately, God's Protestant Message to heathen-turned-Catholic) increased phenomenally during the latter years of the century. From 1870 to 1900 the number of Protestant missions established by Americans abroad increased 500 percent; from 1890 to 1900 the number of American missionaries in China rose from 513 to more than a thousand. Aside from their fund-raising campaigns, which publicized their activities in thousands of American church basements, missionaries also stimulated the growth of American expansionism in other specific ways. Their presence abroad helped American commerce by exposing "natives" to U.S. commodities ordered from home by the missionaries for their own needs. Moreover, many missionaries promoted trade with their converts both for personal profit and moral edification (the classic, if extreme, example was importing American clothing to cover native nakedness; another, more typical, one was encouraging the Christian virtue of frugality by persuading a Samoan to save up for a Singer sewing machine). And—getting back to attitudes—Milton Plesur has noted that the experiences of missionaries tended to erode American parochialism, plant the seeds of internationalism, and arouse a genuine concern for the lives and fortunes, as well as souls, of non-Americans.

The New American Mission. In effect, the missionaries were the first converts to a new definition of the American mission. By the 1890s many articulate Americans were dissatisfied with the passive idea that the United States should provide a model, and nothing more, for others. At a time when the world was smaller and more hazardous than ever and America's moral and material superiority seemed no longer a goal for the future but an established fact, the passivity of the old idea of mission struck many as both a dangerous luxury and a selfish abnegation of duty. "The mission of this country," former Secretary of State Richard Olney wrote in 1898, "is not merely to pose but to act . . . to forego no fitting opportunity to further the progress of civilization." The Wilsonian vision of saving the world for democracy was just around the corner; in the meantime, American ideology had already taken a step that echoed with expansionist resonance.

Journalism and Information. Some Americans, of course, were not seduced by these new fashions in strategy and ideology, but they found themselves hampered in making their case to others by the sparseness of their knowledge about the outside world. They knew relatively little about a place like China and could speak convincingly only about American traditions and principles. The reading public, which had been greatly enlarged by educational advances and now had access to a lengthening list of informative and inexpensive magazines and newspapers, was learning more than ever about the outside world, and in most cases from writers who favored a more adventurous U.S. foreign policy. American journalism on the Far East, for instance, improved markedly after the Sino-Japanese War. "In the earlier period," Marilyn B. Young writes, "journals carried fairly regular articles describing the customs, manners, and general oddities of the mysterious Orient. From 1894 on, these capsule culture essays virtually disappear," to be replaced by "political, social, and economic reports and analyses by a new group of amateur and professional Far Eastern experts."

THE NEW PARADIGM

The net effect of these many developments—both sudden and gradual, domestic and foreign—was the emergence of a new epoch in American foreign policy, the New Paradigm. The American people had not only moved into a world much altered in recent times, but had also come to view their world, and even those parts that had *not* changed, from a radically transformed perspective. They were like valley dwellers forced to move to the mountaintop following a flood; the river bed itself was changed along with other topographical features, and even the little village left behind, although untouched by the deluge, looked remarkably different from the new mountain vantage point. The

New Paradigm was the product of just such a combination of altered landscape and novel perspective, as we shall see from examining its component parts.

The Idea of World Power. In the era of the New Paradigm Americans thought of the United States not merely as a great moral force, but as a world power obligated to act like one. Only a few years earlier U.S. ministers had spent their time agonizing about how best to maintain a simple "republican" style in their residences, dress, and discourse. Now, with unwonted formality and seriousness, they devoted their energies to protecting America's interests and increasing her international influence. This new consciousness of American strength found perfect, and symbolic, expression in the conduct of the U.S. commissioners at the first session of the Paris peace negotiations with Spain in the autumn of 1898. One U.S. delegate, Whitelaw Reid, recorded the event in his diary: ". . . we all entered the large room. Secretary [of State William] Day was taking a place on the side facing the windows, when some of our Commissioners beckoned to him to take the other side, evidently preferring to make the Spaniards face the light."

Expansion of Interests. Aside from tempting Americans to rub salt in the wounds of a onetime power now fallen on hard times, the consciousness of power greatly increased the number of events abroad that officials felt had a direct impact on American interests. They gave close scrutiny not only to such traditional focuses of interest as Canada, Mexico, Cuba, and Hawaii, but also to Nicaragua, Venezuela, Brazil, Chile, China, the Philippines, and even (for a moment) Turkish Armenia. In the easygoing days of the Old Paradigm only a crank would have seen anything "vital" to the United States outside the immediate neighborhood of the nation's borders, but in the 1890s steady-headed American officials detected serious threats to American interests all over the world. Like young men who had put away their toy guns for real weapons, American policymakers put gentler times behind them and girded themselves for a long struggle with what they took to be harsh reality.

Policy. Protecting vital interests in an extended portion of a dangerous world required a real "foreign policy," and its development (within the limits discussed below) was perhaps the most important feature of the New Paradigm. This "policy" approach to diplomacy meant introducing several new characteristics into American diplomatic practice. One was continuity. Abrupt and casual shifts in U.S. policies diminished strikingly in the 1890s. For instance, had Grover Cleveland remained in office after 1897, it seems highly probable that he would have gone to war over Cuba just as McKinley did since he and his successor pursued nearly identical Cuban policies. (LaFeber in *The New Empire* deduces Cleveland's proneness to intervention mainly from his general thesis on the foreign policy consensus of the 1890s, and H. Wayne Morgan in *America's Road to Empire* persuasively asserts the same theme of Cleveland-McKinley continuity, but bases it on other grounds. The thesis has been most convincingly argued, with plentiful documentary support, in Margaret E. Kless, "The Second Grover Cleveland Administration and Cuba: A Study of Policy and Motivation, 1895–1897," M.A. Thesis, The American University, 1970.) Once policymakers identified important American interests abroad, they quickly formulated policies designed for the protection and advancement of those interests, and such rationally constructed policies tended to remain in effect far longer than the spasmodic formulations of former times.

"Policy" also meant a new awareness of the interlacing of issues. The Bering Straits on Tuesday and Hawaii on Wednesday, with a separate folder for each placed on the secretary of state's desk for study, was less the way of doing things in the nineties. How tender would the French, Russians, and British be toward America's interests in distant China if they saw the United States dealing pusillanimously with nearby Cuba? If maintaining American influence in the Far East meant having a navy large and mobile enough to shift on call from Atlantic to Pacific stations, then an isthmian canal controlled by the United States was imperative, and that in turn meant at last coming to terms with Great Britain on the canal issue and keeping a watchful eye on German maneuvering in the Caribbean.

Another sign of the switch to "policy" was the increased readiness of the government to move beyond public opinion's demands if necessary to protect American interests, or alternatively to create public support where it had not previously existed. Although amateurish in technique by the standards of our own times, the United States government consciously undertook to generate support for its policies in the Hawaiian revolution of 1893, the Venezuela boundary dispute of 1895–96, and its decision to send troops to hold the Philippines after Dewey's naval victory of 1898—all examples of strong diplomatic (or, in the last-mentioned case, diplomatically significant) actions that were in no way responsive to preexisting public opinion.

The development of a "policy"-oriented diplomacy also meant a shift in the locus of initiative from the field to Washington, where it had always been for the mere taking, since the newly perceived needs of the era demanded centralized attention and energy. Marilyn B. Young, in her *Rhetoric of Empire*, has described this change as it affected Chinese policy as follows: "Individual Americans, diplomats, missionaries, adventurers [until ca. 1895] acted independently of government direction in the belief that personal efforts could have a direct effect on the destiny of nations, even empires. . . . However, as international rivalries increased, the prerequisite for success became strong government backing, not the heroic efforts of an individual, and bold schemes on the part of restless Americans disappeared. Government initiative replaced that of the individual and, by the end of the first decade of the twentieth century, roles had been so far reversed that the government found itself looking for individual support rather than the other way around." An analogous shift in initiative occurred in economic affairs, a shift not only from the field to Washington, but, to an unprecedented degree, from the private to the public sector. In 1889 the secretary of agriculture implored the Department of State to take "especial pains" in encouraging U.S. consuls to ferret out new markets for American farm commodities, and in 1897 the State Department ordered consuls to give equal attention to "extending the sales of American manufacturers." In 1895 minister to China Charles Denby finally received the free hand he had long demanded in helping American investors and concessions-seekers. In the past he had been required to submit every business proposition to Washington for approval before using his influence to support it, but now Denby—informed that his government expected Americans to receive "equal and liberal trading advantages" in China and Korea— was not only free to do "all" he could "to secure expanded privileges of intercourse, trade and residence" for Americans, but was under orders from Washington to do so. At last he had carte blanche to help any American businessman he found worthy of support. The diplomatic conduct of the United States, though still timid compared with that of many European governments, had come a long way from its former casualness.

In their most ambitious moments, American officials in the era of the New Paradigm were even inclined, when opportunity offered, to use U.S. influence in various balance-of-power situations to promote American interests in a truly farsighted way. And this in turn meant that the United States was now prepared to intervene periodically in the internal affairs of other nations, the sign of a country that takes its foreign policy seriously. As Assistant Secretary of State John Bassett Moore wrote in 1899, the United States had moved "from a position of comparative freedom from entanglements into the position of what is commonly called a world power. . . . Where formerly we had only commercial interests, we now have territorial and political interests as well." Perhaps the greatest sign of the seriousness of a nation's foreign policy is the willingness to use force in its behalf. By this standard, too, the United States government, with its increased tendency to use naval and military force when diplomacy failed, had broken with the past.

Instruments of Foreign Affairs. To support the new foreign policy that extended the frontier of American defense from the Windward Passage to the Heavenly City of Peking, Congress continued to expand and rebuild the navy. It declared in 1899 that all future battleships should possess "great radius of action," and the navy symbolically dropped the term "coast line battleship" from its vocabulary in 1900. The army, however, did not increase its numbers until war actually broke out in 1898. And, although some abler diplomats began representing the United States abroad during the nineties and the rank of ambassador was finally introduced in 1893, significant professionalism in the diplomatic service was still to come.

Limitations of the New Paradigm. The changes we have described were qualified in several important ways. The new diplomatic paradigm did not totally dominate the conduct and thoughts of U.S. officials in the nineties for extended and unbroken periods of time. The decade, in fact, can best be understood as a transitional one, removed in time and style from the age of Hayes and Garfield but just as removed from the extraordinary and bold era of Woodrow Wilson. This is apparent when one considers the sharp geographic limitations of the New Paradigm. The American "defense perimeter" of 1900 may have extended to the China Sea, but it did not reach the English Channel, and certainly not the Rhine. In the nineties the new definition of U.S. policy applied almost exclusively to relations with Latin America and East Asia. Africa was still the Dark Continent, and nonintervention in intrinsically European affairs remained an unchallenged maxim of U.S. diplomacy. This is further confirmation that diplomatic paradigms reflect the obsessions and fantasies of an age every bit as much as the so-called "objective circumstances"; hindsight reveals that American business and security interests in the late 1890s hinged far more on what happened in Europe than Asia, but exactly the reverse seemed true to the men who viewed world affairs through the paradigm filter of that time. Once more it is Professor Young who has made the appropriate observation that Americans in the 1890s "somehow came to feel that having influence in Asia was a categorical imperative for a world power. America was a world power, therefore it must take a key part in Far Eastern affairs *despite an insufficiency of concrete interests that might impel and support such a role*" (my emphasis). In the era of the Old Paradigm, relations with nearly all foreign powers were minimized; under the New Paradigm, America's relations with the Far East were radically altered and her traditional concern with Latin America intensified, but her relationship with Europe and Africa remained for all purposes unchanged.

The new approach to foreign policy met considerable resistance and indifference at home. The economic crisis of the mid-nineties, for example, inspired many solutions—protectionism, trade unionism, socialism, evangelical revivalism, and free silver, to name a few—besides that of boosting exports. Some of America's most astute leaders of business and government were uncertain about the proper course of U.S. foreign policy, and the general public so little understood some of the new diplomatic advances that officials found it necessary to disguise them in the rhetorical garb of the Old Paradigm. Congress at times remained stubbornly old-fashioned and resistant to the new order, scuttling important trade agreements and questioning the wisdom of other new diplomatic initiatives. Those who supported naval reconstruction were not all dedicated Mahanites; many were merely aware that such a building program would produce a healthy din in their districts' shipyards, fire the hearths in underemployed steel mills, or consume enough government revenue to justify the continuation of current protectionist tariff rates. And there were always the anti-imperialists in and out of Congress who rejected the new diplomatic order out of hand, as we shall see in greater detail in Chapter Five.

American diplomats remained distinctly amateurish at times, even those assigned to supposedly crucial posts. The responsibility for appointing them rested with the president himself. McKinley, for instance, made several weak appointments to foreign posts, just as, for domestic political reasons, he named the bumbling Russell Alger head of the War Department and the semisenile John Sherman secretary of state at a time when it was already obvious that a war with Spain might be the major event of his administration.

Behavior, more than rhetoric, is the real measure of a paradigm, and there were times in the 1890s when American diplomatic behavior was as timid, diffuse, and inept as it had ever been. Even though the era closed with the acquisition of a new empire, Washington's administration of these possessions, allegedly so essential to American welfare, was strangely lax and almost forgetful in the years immediately following their acquisition, as demonstrated in Whitney T. Perkins's excellent but little-known book, *Denial of Empire: The United States and Its Dependencies* (1962). Even in China, where the New Paradigm dictated heavy involvement in the years 1895-1900, the conduct of the newcomers to world power seemed halting and inexpert compared to the performance of Europeans, in part because American businessmen searching for profits and diplomats pursuing influence rarely got together to coordinate their efforts. As to the use of force, Warren I. Cohen has observed in a recent synthesis on Chinese-American relations that while the United States was ready enough at this time to engage in rough play against the Chinese (and, we should add, the Filipinos), it never seriously considered unsheathing its sword against Japan or the European powers prominent on the Asian scene (*America's Response to China: An Interpretative History of Sino-American Relations* [1971]). Actually, one gets the impression that American leaders feared they had gotten in over their heads, especially during the Filipino Insurrection and the Boxer Rebellion. During the complex multinational negotiations that followed the rebellion, America's chief delegate, W. W. Rockhill, wrote: "I am sick and tired of the whole business and heartily glad to get away from it. . . . England has her agreement with Germany, Russia has her alliance with France, and the Triple Alliance comes in here [China], and every other combination you know of is working here just as it is in Europe. I trust it may be a long time before the United States gets into another muddle of this description." This sounded more like the utterance of a holdover from the past than an architect of the New Paradigm. Like many Americans of the time, he was probably something of both.

Despite these limitations, American foreign policy had changed significantly by the early nineties. The United States was now assumed to be a major, even an imperial, power. Hence the necessity of having "policies." A Far Eastern policy was essential—all major powers had one. So was a powerful navy. Under the influence, direct or indirect, of the New Paradigm, American statesmen were suddenly entreating their countrymen not to take George Washington's Farewell Address too literally. They still preferred to act unilaterally when possible, but they were willing to cooperate with other powers—especially with an increasingly friendly and respectful Great Britain—if the old ways of doing things seemed inappropriate. From an almost total noninterventionism they plunged into widespread interventionism—in Samoa, Chile, Hawaii, Brazil, Nicaragua, Venezuela, Cuba, Puerto Rico, the Philippines, and China.

We always hunt for symbols of important historical change. It was more than symbolic that while no U.S. troops were serving outside the national boundaries in 1870, 1880, or 1890, they were fighting, standing guard, and even performing the duties of government in Cuba, Puerto Rico, the Philippines, and China by 1900. Surely a new day had dawned.

FOUR

Early Years of the New Era, 1889–1897

BENJAMIN HARRISON

The administration of President Benjamin Harrison, which came into office in March 1889, bore many of the earmarks of the New Paradigm. The president and his secretaries of state, James G. Blaine and John W. Foster (the grandfather of John Foster Dulles), barely dampened their toes in the turbulent waters of East Asia, but in the Western Hemisphere and Central Pacific they plunged spiritedly into the deep. Benjamin Harrison, the shrewd and unfriendly little lawyer from Indiana, was in charge, and although none of his biographers has ever explained how he managed to acquire such a thorough grasp of the foundations of American imperialism, acquire it he did. With unusual bipartisan support in Congress, he was a leader by force of ideas and purpose, not personality. From the start he determined to get "larger markets," especially for American agricultural products; Blaine used the fascinating phrase, "annexation of trade," to describe the administration's objectives.

Both Harrison's singleminded pursuit of commercial, as opposed to colonial, goals and his inquiet conscience on questions of means kept him from a Grant-like policy of "grab" (and also explain why he later became an anti-imperialist). "You know I am not much of an annexationist," he wrote Blaine in 1891, "though I do feel that in some directions, as to naval stations and points of influence, we must look forward to a departure from the too conservative opinions which have been held heretofore." What he apparently had in mind was the acquisition of a few naval harbors and islands in the Gulf of Mexico and the Pacific to ring the site of the still-unbuilt isthmian canal. His was an administration with unusually well defined goals and plans, yet as it turned out these carefully laid plans were eventually disarranged by a series of startling and unplanned incidents.

Trade and Ports.   Harrison and Blaine had little success in their efforts to increase American naval and commercial strength. Harrison, Secretary of the Navy Benjamin F. Tracy, and Congress fostered the new Naval War College, prepared the way for Mahan to indoctrinate its students, and accelerated the ongoing naval construction program; according to one estimate, the U.S. Navy, which ranked somewhere between twelfth and seventeenth among the world's navies in 1889, had moved up to seventh by 1893 and was continuing to rise rapidly. But the attempt to obtain a canal and naval bases failed. In 1891 Harrison asked Congress to guarantee the bonds of a private

American firm set up in 1887 to build a canal through Nicaragua, but nothing came of this venture. The only success that emerged from a flurry of activity aimed at obtaining naval bases was the three-way protectorate over Samoa negotiated in 1889, the credit for which properly belongs to the Cleveland administration. Negotiations to lease the Peruvian port of Chimbote stalled when Peru asked for protectoratelike guarantees of its territory, were further delayed while the United States measured the effects of its 1891–92 crisis with neighboring Chile, and then simply dissolved for lack of interest. In the Caribbean, Harrison and Blaine toyed with reviving Seward's aborted plan to purchase the Danish West Indies and tried without success to lease Samaná Bay in the Dominican Republic. It was in Haiti that they came closest to achieving their goal.

Not without getting embroiled in a local civil war, as events turned out. Grover Cleveland, worried by the European (especially French) support enjoyed by the supposedly legitimate government of Haiti, had flirted with rebels in the north led by Florvil Hyppolite. The latter hinted at one point that U.S. help might be rewarded with a handsome dividend in the form of the port of Môle St. Nicholas, which commanded the strategic Windward Passage between Haiti and Cuba. During its early months in office the Harrison administration made sharp demands on the southern regime, was rebuffed, and then watched with satisfaction as supplies reached Hyppolite's forces from the United States and the rebels seized control of the government in October 1889. Now the United States would receive its dividend. Once in power, however, Hyppolite was not the suppliant he had been in leaner times. He stalled despite pressure from Blaine's agents and a show of U.S. naval force early in 1891, assuming that Harrison was only bluffing. He was right. Harrison did not choose to use naked force and thus forfeited a naval base in Haiti (Ludwell L. Montague, *Haiti and the United States, 1714–1938* [1940]; Allan B. Spetter, "Harrison and Blaine: Foreign Policy, 1889–1893," *Indiana Magazine of History*, LXV, September, 1969). His administration rejected the chance to acquire naval facilities from Portugal in Lisbon, the

Azores, Angola, or Mozambique in the Indian Ocean because its was not the randomly expansionist Old-Paradigm policy of an earlier era, and none of the proposed locations fitted its overall strategy.

Ambitious plans to expand U.S. exports in South and Central America, designed both to promote the American economy and to forestall European political encroachments in the area, gained little ground. One reason for the relatively small commercial traffic between the United States and Latin America was the pathetic condition of American merchant shipping, and Harrison tried to remedy this situation by asking Congress to grant subsidies to mail-carrying ships and bounties to vessels built in the U.S. for use in foreign commerce. Congress, however, produced only modest mail subsidies in response. An initiative that seemed more promising was the Pan-American Conference of 1889-90, the first of its kind ever held. Blaine's original plans for an inter-American meeting had been revived while the Democrats held office. Cleveland issued invitations for the gathering in 1888, and it convened in Washington in October 1889, fittingly presided over by Blaine. He was eager to attack Britain's continued domination of Latin American export markets by persuading the conference participants to establish a customs union with common tariffs against outsiders and preferentially lowered duties within the union. Enthusiastic support for the idea came from important sectors of American manufacturing, agriculture, and shipping, some of whose leaders served as members of the U.S. delegation. Aside from his commercial objectives, Blaine also hoped to emerge from the conference with arbitration machinery for the elimination of armed conflict among hemispheric states. This to Blaine would be both a "realistic" accomplishment in reducing opportunities for European intervention and an "idealistic" one in banishing balance-of-power diplomacy from the hemisphere.

The delegates made a whirlwind tour through major industrial cities to advertise U.S. products to the Latin visitors and publicize the conference to the American people and then settled down for several months' work in November 1889. The results, however, were a great disappointment. Both Argentina and Chile were suspicious, aloof, and generally uncooperative, and most of the other countries present were reluctant to move as fast as the United States wanted. The American public itself grew impatient and critical of so much talk to so little purpose. When the conference finally closed, it had established neither a customs union nor apparatus for arbitration. The conferees suggested that those interested make reciprocal trade agreements bilaterally on their own, and Blaine negotiated several in the next year or so that showed promise, but the new Cleveland administration allowed them to lapse before their effectiveness could be properly tested. Many lesser agreements were never ratified by the Latin American governments. Thus, aside from establishing a precedent for later meetings (a second conference met in Mexico City in 1901) and creating the Bureau of the American Republics (later called the Pan American Union) to serve as a clearing house for information, the long-awaited conference came and went without accomplishing anything significant.

New Orleans, Valparaiso, and Honolulu: Crises in Three Cities. The reputation for cooperation and friendly behavior that America's role in the inter-American conference helped to foster was soon largely nullified by three tumultuous episodes that followed. The first arose in March 1891 when a jury in New Orleans acquitted eleven Italians, suspected of having Mafia connections, of charges of having murdered the local police superintendent. Immediately thereafter a local mob, without interference from the police, tore the prisoners from their jail cells and lynched them. The Italian government demanded redress and punishment of the offenders, but Blaine disclaimed any responsibility on the grounds that the U.S. federal system gave him no authority to act in a local law-enforcement problem. When Italy found this unsatisfactory, he responded with a bombastic lecture on American civics and in effect told the Italians to take it or leave it. Rome recalled its minister to the United States, Washington reciprocated in kind, and in both countries men talked of war. But the Italians cooled off on learning that only three of the victims were still Italian citizens at the time of their deaths. Harrison inserted a tacit apology in his annual message and Blaine quietly sent $25,000 to the bereaved families in Italy from the State Department's secret service fund, thus avoiding a request for funds from Congress. The incident became a memory— but in many countries the recollection was not flattering to the United States.

A second crisis that added to Uncle Sam's saber-rattling image and gave Americans their first real war scare since the *Virginius* affair of 1873 sprang from an incident that occurred in October 1891 in Valparaiso, Chile; 117 American sailors on shore leave from the U.S.S. *Baltimore* were attacked in a drunken brawl in which two Americans were killed, seventeen injured, and many others beaten while Valparaiso police (like their counterparts in New Orleans) merely looked on before finally jailing the remnant. Perhaps drunken tars could expect no better treatment, although in the opinion of one U.S. naval officer the Americans "were probably drunk on shore, properly drunk; they went ashore, many of them, for the purpose of getting drunk, which they did on Chilean rum paid for with good United States money. When in this condition they were more entitled to protection than if they had been sober." Rigidly self-justifying attitudes on both sides pushed the brawl-turned-crisis to the brink of war before it was settled. Relations between the two nations had long been poor. Chile in 1891 needed no reminder that Harrison's secretary of state was the same "Jingo Jim" Blaine who had tried to strip away her territorial gains from the War of the Pacific. An even fresher memory was of America's role in Chile's recent revolution, concluded less than two months before the Valparaiso affray with the victory of the "Congressionalists" over President Balmaceda. The United States had made several cardinal errors—supporting the "unprogressive" cause of executive power against a "parliamentary" claim to power; ineptly offering to mediate the conflict at the very moment the rebels were triumphing; attempting to seize a rebel ship that, according to a subsequent U.S. court decision, was legitimately shipping arms purchased in the United States to

Chile; and giving Balmacedists asylum in the U.S. legation after their defeat—but the worst error, needless to say, had been to back the loser. Shortly after the Congressionalists took power, Harrison described them as ignorant of "how to use victory with dignity and moderation," added that "sometime it may be necessary to instruct them," and saw to it that the United States was slow in recognizing the new government.

Why so much hostility? Wounded pride on both sides, of course, was part of it. Furthermore, Chile's traditional stiff-necked independence grated on American sensibilities more in the nineties than earlier because of the ties between the victorious Congressionalists and Great Britain, now perceived as a threat to vital U.S. interests. With both countries as touchy as rejected lovers, it was no wonder that the Valparaiso affair produced an explosion in U.S.–Chilean relations. Chile's initial reaction was studiously unapologetic, and Harrison threatened retaliation in his annual message of December 9, 1891 (the same one in which he mollified the ruffled Italians). This in turn led to gratuitous insults of Harrison and his administration by the Chilean foreign minister, and the Americans howled for reprisal. One of the dead sailors lay in state in Philadelphia's Independence Hall, an honor accorded only to Clay and Lincoln in the past. Harrison sent Chile an ultimatum on January 21, 1892, threatening a rupture in diplomatic relations unless Chile immediately apologized and made appropriate amends. Suddenly realizing its danger, Chile framed a conciliatory reply that Washington received on January 26, a day after the impatient Harrison had sent Congress a tacit invitation to declare war. Chile's message, which satisfied even Harrison, was an abject apology and promise of indemnity (later set at $75,000) for the injured seamen and families of the dead.

Blaine lay ill during the crisis, barely able to drag himself to the White House a few times to counsel moderation. The navy clearly thirsted for conflict and solemnly estimated the relative advantages of attacking Iquique or Lota (years later a list of "vessels ready in view of possible service against Chile" was found in the personal papers of Secretary of the Navy Tracy).

Harrison himself was in charge throughout, drafting the corre-spondence and ultimatums. At the root of his pugnacity was a hypersensitive national pride and a former soldier's determina-tion to avenge an insult to the American uniform. But though these were Harrison's personal motives, his conduct of the affair was completely consistent with the general spirit of the New Paradigm: foreign influence in the hemisphere was considered dangerous, events in faraway countries (even internal politics) were vitally important to the United States, and threatening to use armed force was an acceptable American diplomatic weapon. The consequences of the affair were a further embitter-ment of Chile toward the United States, a blow against the brotherly spirit of the recent Pan-American conference, a growing suspicion of Yankee diplomacy in other Latin Ameri-can capitals, and a vigorous stoking of the fires of nationalism at home. (The details will be found in Frederick B. Pike, *Chile and the United States, 1880–1962* [1963], which places less emphasis on economic matters than LaFeber's account in *The New Empire.* The same is true of Spetter's "Harrison and Blaine" article mentioned earlier and A. T. Volwiler, "Harrison, Blaine, and American Foreign Policy, 1889–1893," American Philo-sophical Society *Proceedings*, LXXIX, 1938.)

The final and most important diplomatic venture of the Harrison administration was the sudden attempt to annex Hawaii in 1893. With the Bering Sea controversy stilled in the north and the Samoan question temporarily settled in the south, the stage was set to complete America's Pacific picket line in Hawaii. The influence of American settlers had continued to grow since renewal of the reciprocal trade agreement in 1887, but a new mainland duty on Hawaiian sugar dealt a heavy blow to their sector of the islands' economy in 1890. Aware that annexation would bring them directly inside the U.S. tariff wall—though it would also mean abolition of Hawaii's contract-labor system—the Americans and their European allies in Hawaii grew increasingly proannexation and aggressive in wielding their influence locally. The young Queen Liliuokalani responded with a reassertion of her own monarchical prerogatives and the primacy of Hawaiian interests. Angered, the Americans decided to depose her, proclaim a republic, and seek immediate annexation to the United States. But they needed help. It was forthcoming from the expansionist U.S. Minister John L. Stevens, whose intervention in January 1893 surpassed their wildest hopes. Acting swiftly and on his own authority, Stevens promised military support to Liliuokalani's rebellious subjects, ordered 150 marines from an offshore naval vessel to guard locations in Honolulu that the rebels would have to control in order to carry out their *coup,* stood by contentedly while the rebels deposed the Queen and proclaimed a republic, recognized the new regime before Liliuokalani's main defense forces had had a chance to surrender, declared an American protectorate over Hawaii, and raised the U.S. flag over Honolulu. Washington disavowed the protectorate, but nothing else. In fact, Secretary of State Foster was soon discussing terms of annexation with a delegation from Hawaii's provisional government (which, incidentally, included no Hawaiians). They completed their work February 14, and President Harrison, though lukewarm to the idea (George W. Baker, Jr., "Benjamin Harrison and Hawaiian Annexation: A Reinterpretation," *Pacific Historical Review,* XXXIII, August 1964), sent the treaty to the Senate on the fifteenth, only thirty days after Stevens had called out the marines and started the ball rolling.

The Senate however, slowed down proceedings because of its own doubts and President-elect Cleveland's request for delay. Cleveland smelled a rat, or at least a thickening plot, and, always suspicious of Republican diplomacy, ordered former Democratic Congressman James H. Blount of Georgia to investigate Stevens's shenanigans. Once in Hawaii, Blount returned the marines to their ship, lowered the American flag, and reported to Cleveland that the revolution would never have come off without Stevens's illicit meddling. Cleveland first tried to restore Queen "Lil" to her throne, found that effort both impractical and unpopular, and then dropped the whole matter in the lap of Congress, which did nothing at all.

Despite its inconclusive outcome, the Hawaiian affair was

significant in several respects. It sparked an important public debate on expansion, and it accentuated policy differences between Cleveland and the Republicans, who now became more consciously expansionist than ever. The incident also underlined the transitional nature of the paradigm change at the time. In Old Paradigm fashion, American involvement originated not in Washington, but in Honolulu; Stevens's only "expansionist" instructions were to secure U.S. cable-landing rights in Hawaii. But the brisk way in which the Harrison administration pounced on its sudden opportunity was a sign of the times. The administration took such bold action for several definite reasons: concern about British and Japanese influence in Hawaii, interest in securing important economic benefits for the United States, and conviction that control of Hawaii would protect American shipping lanes to Asia and defend a future isthmian canal from any naval threat based in the Pacific.

GROVER CLEVELAND

Cleveland's handling of the Hawaii affair reveals much about his approach to foreign policy. He was an unbending foe of annexing new territory. Bringing the dark-skinned Hawaiians into the Republic had no appeal for him. He could be a stern moralist. Though capable of using foreign policy for partisan ends, this mountainous and unshakable man could withstand great popular pressure without flinching. But, at the same time, he could be clumsy and even irresponsible, as witnessed by his chronic invitations to Congress to make the next move toward some goal he refused to define. The return to power of this staunch traditionalist, however, did not signal a retreat to the Old Paradigm, as his Hawaiian policy makes clear. For he, like so many of his countrymen, had come to take a different view of the importance of foreign affairs since his first term as president in the eighties. He continued to oppose the annexation of Hawaii, ever mindful that the Republicans had first attempted it, but he was assiduous in seeing to it that American influence remained dominant in the islands. And in Latin America his diplomacy in the years 1893–97 became progressively more deliberate, aggressive, and expansionist.

In European matters, however, American policy under Cleveland remained quiet and uninvolved, and intervention in the Far East seemed even more distasteful to him than in Hawaii. Secretary of State Walter Q. Gresham characterized the Sino-Japanese War as nothing for Americans to trouble themselves about, and at its conclusion Cleveland proudly reported that, on the one occasion when the United States had offered help in inaugurating peace talks, it had "sought no advantages and interposed no counsels." Some officials did worry that a weakened China might become easy prey for rapacious imperialists, but they did nothing about it at the time. The Far Eastern piece in the design of the New Paradigm had not yet been put in place.

Walter LaFeber has described Cleveland's energetic Western Hemisphere policy as "depression diplomacy," a concerted effort to bring the United States out of the slough of depression by the aggressive expansion of exports. Others explain it as politics, an attempt from the autumn of 1893 onward to save Cleveland from a reputation for timidity in foreign affairs (e.g., Nelson M. Blake, "Background of Cleveland's Venezuela Policy," *American Historical Review*, XLVII, January 1942). Both explanations are too narrow. Many factors were at work—all the elements, in fact, of the New Paradigm. Although Cleveland formed his Latin American policy in response to a series of discrete incidents, the results show that his administration was moving in the direction of an overall objective: staving off European threats to American political and economic influence in the Caribbean and along the northern shores of South America.

Minor Crises in the Hemisphere. Three examples of Cleveland's dealings with Latin America deserve brief mention. The first was his intervention in Brazil's civil war in 1893. The contest pitted the established government against rebels supporting a return to monarchical government. The United States disapproved of the moral support Germany and other European countries were giving the rebels but was not eager to interfere. Washington did, however, reject requests from the rebels to recognize their belligerency and the legitimacy of their proclaimed blockade of Rio de Janeiro, the purpose of which was to deny the government essential supplies and customs revenues. The United States sent warships to support its insistence on the right of American goods to enter the harbor, and one fired on an obstructive rebel ship while escorting a merchant vessel to dock. The insurgency eventually petered out, in part because of Washington's firmness on the blockade question. Neither the Cleveland administration nor the American public had found the affair especially significant (Lawrence F. Hill, *Diplomatic Relations Between the United States and Brazil* [1932]).

In 1894, this time in Central America, the United States became mildly entangled in events arising from Nicaragua's decision to impose its sovereignty over the Mosquito Indian Reservation, technically independent but for a third of a century the ward of Great Britain. The idea of Queen Victoria protecting the Mosquito Indians in Central America was the sort of thing Englishmen could be quite solemn about in those days, and Great Britain quickly sent some of her soldiers to disarm the upstart Nicaraguans. As described in Walter LaFeber's *The New Empire*, the United States reacted by supporting Nicaragua's stand and successfully maneuvered "England out of its strategic position. . . ." Certainly the quickening interest in commerce and an isthmian canal gave Americans reason to welcome Britain's departure, but actually no important Anglo-American conflict was involved: the British left contentedly once the United States government assured them that the Indians' rights would not be abused. Nicaragua formally incorporated the territory in December, about the time of another contretemps in British-Nicaraguan relations—the Corinto Affair. This was a trivial episode named for the Nicaraguan port occupied by the British after the arrest and deportation of one of their consular officers; it is important only because of what it reveals about American public opinion at the time. England demanded an apology and indemnity, and the panicky Nicaraguans appealed to Washington for help: please, they cried, uphold the Monroe Doctrine! Cleveland and Gresham did nothing, however, because they believed Britain had a right to punish the errant Nicaraguans and was in no way jeopardizing the Monroe Doctrine. British forces left after settlement of the affair in the spring of 1895, but long into the summer many Americans were still excoriating Cleveland with unbridled fervor for his inaction.

The Venezuela Affair.   The Venezuela Crisis of 1895–96 has always been something of a puzzle to students of Cleveland's second administration. The bone of contention was the fifty-year old dispute over the boundary between Venezuela and British Guiana, which involved hundreds of thousands of acres of land and a sizable population, the mouth of the Orinoco River with its potential for tapping the commerce of the interior of South America, and gold fields in which the largest gold nugget in the world had recently been discovered. For many years the Venezuelans had asked for arbitration of the dispute, only to be refused by the haughty British, who were in no mood to establish an inconvenient legal precedent that would cast doubt on the boundaries of their many other colonial possessions. Cleveland had been aware of the issue for some time and had vainly supported Venezuela's proposal for arbitration on three occasions prior to 1895, once as early as 1887 during his first administration. The American public, however, was not generally aware of the dispute until the early months of 1895 when Congress passed resolutions in favor of arbitration. The press then picked up the issue, and by summertime a few already sensed a diplomatic donnybrook in the offing.

Cleveland decided to press the issue and put Secretary Gresham to work composing a message to London. But Gresham died suddenly, and the dispatch was finished by his successor, former Attorney General Richard Olney, a stern Boston lawyer who had just sent Eugene Debs to prison for his part in the Pullman Boycott and who had years earlier banished his own daughter from his home, never to see her again although they both lived in the same city for thirty years. Cleveland himself was not timorous when it came to severity; he closely scrutinized and completely approved everything that followed. Olney's note was slightly modified and sent to Britain on July 20, 1895. It was an amazing document. Not only did Olney use belligerent language in demanding the submission of the dispute to international arbitration, but he buttressed his case with variations on the Monroe Doctrine that must surely have caused the fifth President to turn in his grave, including the famous passage: "Today the United States is practically sovereign on this continent, and its fiat is law upon the subjects to which it confines its interposition . . . because, in addition to all other grounds, its infinite resources combined with its isolated position render it master of the situation and practically invulnerable as against any or all other powers."

Cleveland hoped for Britain's reply in time to comment on it in his annual December message, but due to administrative oversights and a miscalculation of Washington's attitude, the response of Prime Minister Salisbury (who doubled as his own foreign minister) was exasperatingly slow in arriving. As a result, Cleveland's December 2 message merely recapitulated recent events, gave a blatantly anti-British analysis of the boundary dispute, and reaffirmed his insistence on arbitration. Five days later Salisbury's reply arrived. His arrogance a worthy match for Olney's belligerence and his manner that of a schoolmaster explaining simple ideas to simple children, Salisbury rejected Olney's version of the Monroe Doctrine, denied its standing in international law or applicability to the case at hand, heaped contempt on the Venezuelans, and peremptorily rejected the demand for arbitration. Cleveland, now "mad clean through" by his own description, replied in a message to Congress on December 17, 1895, that ranks as one of the greatest bombshells in the history of American foreign relations. In defiant tones he asked Congress for authority to appoint his own commission to determine the proper boundary lines, stipulating that it was America's "duty . . . to resist by every means in its power as a willful aggression upon its rights and interests the appropriation by Great Britain of any lands or the exercise of governmental jurisdiction over any territory which after investigation we have determined of right belongs to Venezuela." The normally phlegmatic President then assured the world that he was "fully alive to the responsibility incurred, and . . . all the consequences that may follow."

Cleveland's bombshell set off a veritable explosion of patriotism and Anglophobia. Congress immediately granted the requested authority. Criticism of Cleveland's action and a brief Wall Street panic (caused mainly by Britishers' unloading of American securities) were overwhelmed by frenzied talk of war—a preview of the hysteria that would mark the Cuban crisis less than three years later. Across the Atlantic, however, most Englishmen were dismayed. A feeling that war between the two great English-speaking nations would be a tragic absurdity began to surface in both countries almost immediately after the first wave of excitement had passed. Then, as negotiations for a settlement were just getting under way, the German Kaiser on January 3, 1896, in a gratuitous and ominous gesture, telegraphed congratulations to President Krüger of the Boer Republic for repelling the "Jameson Raid," staged from neighboring British territory. Venezuela was swept from the front pages in London, and Britain's anger turned toward Germany. Acutely aware of their diplomatic isolation in Europe, the British realized the value of a friendly United States.

The crisis atmosphere was deflated as quickly as it had swelled. Negotiators reached agreement speedily after some lengthy sessions over which issues Britain would or would not submit to arbitration. The results were anticlimactic: a Venezuelan-British treaty of arbitration in 1897 and an award from the arbitrators two years later that supported the principal British claims. By that time no one in the United States cared. Far greater events were occupying the limelight. Besides, Cleveland had made his point.

But what, in fact, was it? Why had the erstwhile mayor of Buffalo thrown the gauntlet at the feet of the Third Marquis of Salisbury? To gain political credit through a vigorous twist of the lion's tail? Perhaps. The final months of 1895 were certainly an opportune time for that game. Cleveland was under heavy attack, mainly from fellow Democrats, for his domestic policies, especially for halting the silver-purchase program and allowing J. P. Morgan's Anglo-American banking syndicate to reap large profits in a less-than-successful effort to shore up the national gold reserves. Irish voters accused him of being a limey-lover. Expansionists of both parties criticized him for diplomatic spinelessness: he had lowered the flag over Hawaii, ignored congressional entreaties to use U.S. influence to end the massacre of Armenians in Turkey, and watched passively while Britain bullied Nicaragua at Corinto. Could he permit further disintegration of his party? Could he afford more diplomatic inactivity? Could he pass up the popularity he might gain from a rousing burst of Anglophobia? As a Democrat from Texas wrote him: "Turn this Venezuela question up or down, North, South, East or West, and it is a 'winner.' "

Cleveland undoubtedly entertained such thoughts, but only with passing effect. He was an unimaginative man, uniformly described by his biographers as mulish, and not the sort to crumple under the weight of crude political pressure. Nearing the end of his second presidential term, he apparently gave no serious thought to running for a third. He could not, at any rate, have believed that his decision on Venezuela would either reunite his party or strengthen his own political position since the people who backed his policy most vocally were either Republican imperialists or Democratic and Populist silverites who considered Cleveland the devil incarnate and, in effect, read him out of the Democratic party several months later by nominating William Jennings Bryan for president.

If politics cannot explain Cleveland's actions, neither can morality. What he knew of the boundary controversy—and his information was both biased and incomplete—outraged his sense of fair play, but if it was fairness in foreign relations he was after, why hadn't he taken up the cudgels for Venezuela back in 1887? Or why hadn't he responded to the flagrant immorality of the Armenian massacres? Because, in response to the first question, British highhandedness in the hemisphere seemed to have far more disturbing implications in 1895 than it had in the eighties; and, in reply to the second, events in faraway Turkey were no threat to the United States. The essential thing for the president was that Venezuela was nearby and—as he saw it—American interests there were directly threatened by British policy.

Cleveland acted on the basis of a highly distorted picture of the boundary dispute, drawn for him by Venezuelan lobbyists. He was not striking out at phantoms, however. British control of the Orinoco and the new gold fields might harm the American economy in the future, but, even more important, it might set off a general European attempt to poach on American grounds. The idea was not fantastic in that golden age of European imperialism. The scramble for empire had been extraordinarily stepped up in the interval between Cleveland's inauguration in March 1893 and his bellicose message on Venezuela in December 1895. In Asia, France had reduced Laos to a protectorate and joined Russia and Germany in forcing Japan to disgorge the mainland gains from her war with China. In Africa, Italy had come to terms with England on the disposition of East Africa and launched a campaign to conquer Ethiopia; Belgium was angling for territory on the Upper Nile; Germany had carved out the boundaries of the Cameroons in agreements with Britain and France; the latter had taken over Guinea, the Ivory Coast, and Dahomey and started the conquest of Madagascar; Britain had made a protectorate of Uganda, occupied Matabeleland, annexed Pondoland and Togoland, organized Rhodesia and the East African Protectorate, and annexed "British" Bechuanaland to her Cape Colony. In the Western Hemisphere, Germany had shown an alarming interest in the attempted Brazilian revolution; France had hectored Santo Domingo with a naval demonstration and—from her base in Guiana—had put forward claims to territory in northwestern Brazil that led to actual fighting between French and Brazilian troops in May 1895; and Great Britain had not only harassed Nicaragua in the Mosquito Reservation and Corinto affairs, but also occupied the islet of Trinidade despite the prior claims of Brazil.

What were Americans to think? What did the altered perspective of the New Paradigm suggest to them? Cleveland and most others had come to think that the insatiably imperialist powers of Europe were taking dangerous liberties in the United States's own sphere of influence. The president was not fretting over the interests of Venezuela, whose government he never consulted during the entire crisis. What worried him was the political, economic, and strategic threat to the United States being fashioned by outside powers. He was determined to quash that threat and secure acknowledgement of America's supremacy in the hemisphere. The grim determination of 1895, which replaced the vague uneasiness of 1887, reflected changes in both landscape and perspective: the European imperialist impulse had gained momentum; the American picture of the world at home and abroad had altered. The United States was more powerful and yet more vulnerable than during Cleveland's first administration. The world beyond San Francisco, New Orleans, and New York was more relevant to America's welfare than before, thus necessitating the forming of "policies." Cleveland was not prepared, as Theodore Roosevelt was in 1904, to lay down a precise definition of future relations among the United States, Latin America, and outside powers, but he knew what he was doing: asserting U.S. supremacy in the New World.

Cuba. This insistence on America's dominant role was also apparent in Cleveland's handling of the rebellion that began in Cuba in February 1895. The new struggle was fed by many of the same grievances that had nourished the Cuban war of 1868–78 and was intensified by a severe depression arising from a 40 percent duty on Cuban sugar sold in the United States (authorized in the same U.S. tariff act of 1894 that lowered duties on Hawaiian sugar). The uprising quickly became a full-blown revolution, and early in 1896 command of Spain's armies was turned over to General Valeriano Weyler, known as "the Butcher" for his tactics in the earlier rebellion. He initiated a ruthless "reconcentration" policy, sweeping peasants into concentration camps to keep them from supplying recruits and material help to the rebel armies. Hunger and disease struck the camps and thousands died. With equal ferocity the insurgents set out to paralyze the island's economy with a scorched-earth strategy, fully aware that many plantations and sugar mills being put to the torch were owned by American citizens who might demand protection from their government and thus provoke U.S. intervention. Working for the rebels' cause within the United States was the Cuban Junta, a large organization of exiles, naturalized U.S. citizens of Cuban birth, and native American sympathizers, which raised money, distributed prorebel copy to newspapers, lobbied vigorously in Washington, and smuggled soldiers and ammunition into Cuba. Newspaper publishers discovered a ready market for sensational Cuban news among a people who had been deeply stirred by the Venezuela crisis and now waited to see what Washington would do about Cuba. Certainly something had to be done! America could not tolerate such barbarities and bloodshed only ninety miles from its shores.

José Martí, the Cuban patriot, had remarked a few years earlier: "Once the United States is in Cuba, who will get her out?" Cleveland, who would have raised the same question, was firmly opposed to annexing Cuba and thus chary of armed intervention. Yet he came extremely close to it as, always wary and never impulsive, he moved gradually from a neutrality that emphasized sympathetic cooperation with Spain to an implicitly prorebel attempt at mediation, and finally to a stern warning that an increasingly impatient America might intervene to defend its carefully defined interests. The first position, which lasted until the spring of 1896, was initially established a year earlier when Washington proclaimed its neutrality and recognized the rebels' status as insurgents, but not belligerents. Though U.S. neutrality laws were difficult to enforce, the administration did as well as could be expected and specifically warned Americans against prorebel activities within the United States. Cleveland and Olney were becoming concerned about damage to American interests in Cuba, but at this stage they accepted the Spanish minister's claim that only the dregs of Cuban society supported the insurrection, which was destined to be short-lived, and even gave Spain friendly encouragement to hurry up the process of suppression.

By the spring of 1896, however, a contrary mood had seized Congress, which passed a concurrent resolution recognizing Cuba's belligerency and urging the president to extract Cuban independence from Spain. Cleveland ignored the resolution but began to change his policy, partly because of congressional pressure but also because of his own shifting evaluation of the rebellion. He now moved to the old Hamilton Fish policy of trying to end the violence by urging Spain to grant substantial concessions to the rebels. Though still unwilling to recognize their belligerency, the Cleveland administration was rapidly coming to the conclusion that the rebellion could not be put down by force. Therefore, in April 1896, Olney urged Spain to make major reforms throughout the island, which he promised the United States would encourage the Cubans to accept. His message listed several reasons for his government's sudden concern: it wanted to spur the development of "free" governments in the hemisphere; put an end to the suffering and tragedies of war; restore trade with Cuba, reduced by half of its normal annual value of $100 million since 1894; and halt the destruction of American investments, worth about $40 million at that time. Besides these ideological, humanitarian, and economic motives specifically mentioned by Olney, the administration was eager to safeguard America's canal prospects and prevent Spain from calling in European help to suppress the rebellion. The McKinley administration would find little to add to this rationale of 1896.

Spain rejected Olney's bid and attempted to build a counterforce of friendly European powers against American pressure. But when the U.S. minister in Spain got wind of the project and protested, it died aborning. U.S.–Spanish relations were obviously deteriorating rapidly as the sands of Cleveland's administration ran out. In his last annual message, on December 2, 1896, President Cleveland went one step further, citing the damage being done to American interests that were "by no means of a wholly sentimental or philanthropic character," implying that the United States no longer believed Spain capable of quelling the rebellion, and advocating Cuban autonomy as a solution. Although he still refrained from recognizing either Cuban belligerency or independence, he warned Spain (and repeated the warning in February 1897) that if the "senseless slaughter" and destruction continued, the United States would have no choice but to intervene directly.

But he would go no further, as was dramatically demonstrated late in December 1896 when he had Olney denounce a resolution to recognize Cuban independence then making its way through Congress. Olney stated that recognition was an executive responsibility and vowed that the administration would completely ignore the measure should it pass. The Capitol Hill initiative collapsed. Cleveland's determination to hold back at this juncture had several causes. He refused to recognize the Cubans' belligerency because he was never convinced they deserved belligerent status and feared recognition would release Spain from her obligation to protect American property in Cuba. Recognition of Cuban independence, which he found even less warranted, might provoke Spain to declare war on the United States. At any rate, it would be tantamount to branding Spain as a violator of the Monroe Doctrine. And Cleveland feared that the war that would almost certainly follow would lead willy-nilly to annexation. In his last days in office Cleveland was particularly reluctant to do anything that would tie the hands of the incoming president before he had a chance to make his own choices. The Spanish-American War was to be McKinley's war, not because Cleveland was an old-fashioned isolationist with a stiffer backbone than his successor, but because he left office without having to face the new problems that soon engulfed McKinley.

FIVE

War, Policy, and Imperialism at the End of the Century, 1897–1900

William McKinley was elected president in 1896 on a platform calling for the vigorous reassertion of the Monroe Doctrine, Cuban independence, a strong navy, control over Hawaii, purchase of the Virgin Islands, "the eventual withdrawal of the European powers from this hemisphere," and "the ultimate union of all English-speaking parts of the continent by the free consent of its inhabitants." When McKinley took office in March 1897, he was hovered over by an eager clique of imperialists: Assistant Secretary of the Navy Theodore Roosevelt, Captain Alfred T. Mahan, Senators Henry Cabot Lodge and Cushman K. Davis, writer Brooks Adams, and others. They were determined to implement what Lodge called "the large policy," defined by historian Julius W. Pratt as a program to make the United States "the indisputably dominant power in the western hemisphere, possessed of a great navy, owning and controlling an Isthmian canal, holding naval bases in the Caribbean and the Pacific, and contesting, on at least even terms with the greatest powers, the naval and commercial supremacy of the Pacific Ocean and the Far East" ("The 'Large Policy' of 1898," *Mississippi Valley Historical Review*, XIX, September 1932).

At least this is how the McKinley story used to begin, but historians have recently corrected the old picture of a passive and rudderless McKinley being pushed toward war and imperialism by an expansionist cabal and an hysterical public, and the new estimate of McKinley strongly supports our picture of decisive diplomatic change in the nineties. Most of the men mentioned above were actually on the margins of power in 1897–98 and not nearly as influential as William R. Day (at first assistant secretary of state, then secretary) and Senators William B. Allison, Stephen B. Elkins, Orville H. Platt, and John C. Spooner (see Horace C. and Marion G. Merrill, *The Republican Command, 1897–1913* [1971]). McKinley himself was far abler than many of his contemporaries (and most historians until recently) realized. This former Civil War major and longtime Ohio politician was not brilliant or especially imaginative, but he was intelligent, unruffled in time of crisis, and effective in getting his own way. He was always a hard man to understand owing to his reticence, oblique way of doing things, and disinclination to commit his thoughts on any important subject to paper. Nonetheless, we now recognize that he was a resourceful political leader and minor master in managing those around him. He needed no advice from others to convince him that the United States should play a greater role in world affairs, both to do good and, as he told Robert La Follette in 1897, to gain "American supremacy in world markets."

WAR AND EMPIRE

McKinley hoped to achieve these ends peacefully but, from the beginning of his administration, he was prepared as a last resort to use force in Cuba. U.S. Minister to Spain Stewart L. Woodford reported in September 1897 that Spain did not have a Cuban "policy." McKinley did, however. The president charted his course cautiously, hoping to avoid a war that would damage the advancing business recovery and spawn its own problems, but by his first autumn in office he was closer to war than Cleveland had ever been, and for two main reasons. First, while Cleveland had long been content with the prospect of Spain's suppressing the rebellion by any means whatever, McKinley's administration as early as June 26, 1897, demanded a speedy end to the "uncivilized and inhumane conduct" of the war. Second, McKinley, unlike Cleveland, made it clear that he would have no part in imposing a settlement on the Cubans that they found unacceptable. The combination of General Weyler's harsh methods and the rebels' refusal to accept even an autonomous status makes it evident in retrospect that by the summer of 1897 the United States and Spain were careening rapidly toward a head-on collision—well before the "yellow" newspaper campaigns for intervention, the de Lôme letter, or the sinking of the *Maine*.

There were, in addition, a number of specific factors that pushed McKinley ever closer to war. The rebellion caused uncertainty in American political and economic life and produced, as the State Department complained in July 1897, "a continuous irritation within our borders"; it might become necessary to impose peace on the island to restore American "tranquillity," if for no other reason. Patrolling the Gulf of Mexico to enforce U.S. neutrality laws and keeping the navy ready for possible action were expensive. Moreover, the longer the Cuban problem remained unresolved the more likely it was that some European power would move menacingly into America's backyard, as Germany did in the winter of 1897 in a belligerent gunboat demonstration against Haiti that was accompanied by denunciations of the Monroe Doctrine and announcement of German plans to build new warships for the Caribbean and South Atlantic. In faraway China Germany seized Kiaowchow in November; it was a disturbing portent, and the United States could do nothing about it as long as Cuba monopolized its attention.

In an effort to appease American displeasure, a new Spanish ministry recalled Weyler, promised an end to the reconcentration policy, and announced a series of reforms in Cuba. But the McKinley administration, growing skeptical of both the sincerity and likely success of Spain's reforms, began clearing the decks for action. In October 1897 the United States warned Spain not to seek help from other European governments, and in his annual message in December McKinley made it clear, though not in so many words, that Spain must reform Cuba from top to bottom or face American intervention.

The pace toward war quickened with the coming of the new year. On January 17 Queen Regent Maria implored U.S. Minister Woodford to ease the pressure on Spain and have faith in her reform intentions. But proarmy and antireform riots in Havana five days before her plea produced a wave of skepticism in Washington. Even if Spain were sincere (which the administration doubted), and even if its promise of Cuban autonomy were genuine (doubtful also since the plan explicitly reserved ultimate authority to Madrid), the Spanish government appeared unable to carry out its Cuban edicts against the will of the army and people. McKinley still hoped to avoid war—he always would—but increasingly doubted his ability to do so. His pessimism was felt across the Atlantic, and Spain moved to a strategy of procrastination—the proverbial "mañanaism"—supplemented by an intensified bid for Big-Power support.

Two great blows rocked Spanish-American relations in

February 1898. The first occurred when a private letter of the Spanish minister to Washington, Enrique Dupuy de Lôme, was intercepted by a Junta member and published in a New York newspaper on February 9. De Lôme's most famous phrase, describing McKinley as "weak and a bidder for the admiration of the crowd," was bad enough, and the hapless minister promptly resigned before the administration could demand his recall. Even more serious in the eyes of American policymakers, however, was evidence in the letter indicating that neither the announced reforms in Cuba nor Spain's concurrent negotiations for a commercial pact with the United States were being carried out in good faith. Spain's apology, moreover, was begrudging and slow in coming. The damage had been done, and now the administration's doubts that Spain could effectually reform Cuba were joined by a disbelief in her good faith. Outside the administration many moderates who felt they had been duped by Spanish treachery came out in favor of armed intervention (see especially H. Wayne Morgan, "The DeLôme Letter: A New Appraisal," *The Historian*, XXVI, November 1963).

Six days after de Lôme's letter was published, the second-class battleship *Maine*, while on a mission that combined goodwill with vigilance, blew up and sank in Havana harbor. Inflamed headlines and mass meetings demanded vengeance for the 260 Americans killed on board. Dissatisfaction with McKinley's imperturbability mounted in Congress. Although the disaster was probably caused by an accident or insurgent sabotage rather than treachery on the part of Spain, which could only lose from the catastrophe, the event contributed more than any other to making war inevitable. McKinley's initial reaction, however, was to order a naval inquiry and avoid all harsh recriminations. He did not allow himself to be stampeded into war by the popular frenzy, as evidenced by the fact that hostilities did not begin until the *Maine* had lain at the bottom of Havana harbor for over two months.

But time *was* running out. The United States informally warned de Lôme's successor in the first week of March that a major crisis was inevitable unless Spain quickly satisfied American demands, including possible U.S. mediation of the rebellion. At the same time, McKinley requested and received from Congress $50 million to get ready for war. On March 17 Senator Redfield Proctor of Vermont, an unflappable moderate who had just returned from a tour of Cuba, made a speech that electrified the country with its description of Spain's cruelties and the failure of her reforms and then called for American intervention. Rumors that McKinley had sent Proctor to Cuba and even cleared his speech prior to delivery augmented its impact on public opinion. A few days later, McKinley's naval board of inquiry informed him that the *Maine* had been sunk by an external explosion, thus ruling out the possibility of an on-board accident. McKinley kept the report secret for a week, perhaps hoping that the threat of its disclosure would force Spain to accept the terms he was then demanding.

These terms were long misunderstood by historians, who argued that McKinley caved in to jingoistic pressure even though Spain at the last moment responded satisfactorily to his demands. But the responses, in fact, were not satisfactory. McKinley's terms, in their final form, were sent to Spain on March 27, 1898, after he had already promised to submit the whole matter to Congress by April 15 unless Madrid satisfied his demands in the meantime. The demands were hard: Spain must declare an immediate armistice that would last until October 1, permanently abolish the reconcentration policy, carry out thorough war-relief measures, and permit the president to mediate the conflict if a settlement between Spain and the rebels was not reached during the armistice. The last item, whose significance many historians have missed—owing perhaps to its vague wording—was McKinley's trump card since it encompassed an implicit demand for Cuban independence should he, in the role of mediator, request it.

Spain's reply, which arrived a few days later, promised total reform of Cuba (how many times had Americans heard that promise in the past thirty years?), an unequivocal end to reconcentration, and an armistice *if the rebels asked for one.* Because such an armistice looked suspiciously like an invitation to the rebels to disarm themselves and because Spain had also rejected mediation, McKinley felt justified in going ahead with his "war" message. But there was a delay while he allowed a few days for evacuation of Americans from Cuba. Marking time, he listened politely on April 7 while a delegation of European ministers and ambassadors relayed their nations' hopes for peace, a *pro forma* affair of little concern to McKinley who correctly sensed that neither Germany nor Britain was prepared to incur American displeasure over the issue. Then, just as the president was about to go ahead with his message, news came that Spain had made a new concession, unilaterally proclaiming an armistice of indefinite length. When Assistant Secretary of State Day asked the Spanish minister whether anything in this last communication could be construed to mean a promise of Cuban independence, the answer was no. No Spanish government could give up Cuba and remain another day in office.

Thus, after nearly three years of diplomatic maneuvering, a dead end. McKinley finally sent his message to Congress on April 11. Like most presidents going to war, he threw in everything but the kitchen sink in his statement of grievances. He then asked for authority to end the Cuban rebellion and, as an afterthought, added a paragraph calling attention to Spain's recent armistice proclamation. For a few days Congress tried to get McKinley to recognize the rebels as the government of Cuba in exchange for support of his requests, but the president wanted a free hand in dealing with the Cubans. In the end a majority in both houses of Congress backed his refusal to accept recognition—strong evidence that he was commanding events and following a calculated line of policy at the very time that historians have traditionally described him as a puppet of congressional and public opinion. A joint congressional war resolution finally emerged on April 19; it proclaimed the end of Spanish sovereignty in Cuba, gave McKinley authority to employ armed force to end the rebellion, and promised in the Teller Amendment that the United States itself would not annex Cuba. By April 25, declarations and counterdeclarations from both countries had brought Spain and the United States into a state of official hostilities. Americans had entered their first foreign war in a half century.

Many of McKinley's contemporaries would have agreed with the historians who held that he was pushed unwittingly into war. Senator John C. Spooner felt that war was avoidable, "but the current was too strong, the demagogues too numerous, the fall elections too near." This view does not hold up under the weight of recent scholarship. McKinley, of course, did not prefer war; few statesmen have said when the fighting was done, "I wanted war." But he did want what only war could bring him—an end to the Cuban rebellion, which outraged his humanitarian impulses, prolonged instability in the economy, destroyed American investments and trade with Cuba, created a dangerous picture of an America unable to master the affairs of the Caribbean, threatened to arouse an uncontrollable outburst of jingoism, and diverted the attention of U.S. policymakers from historic happenings in China (as McKinley confidant Whitelaw Reid wrote: "as soon as Cuba is out of the way the present Chinese complications are likely to develope [sic] a great deal of interest for us"). Only if Spain had surrendered to all of McKinley's demands could war have been prevented, and this was no more in the cards than it was for McKinley in this new era to forget about Cuba altogether. Neither spineless nor bellicose, McKinley demanded what seemed to him morally unavoidable and essential to American interests; for its part, Spain, whose leaders had their own moral and political imperatives, elected war over surrender. (LaFeber in *The New Empire* emphasizes McKinley's economic motives, broadly interpreted; Ernest R. May in *Imperial Democracy: The Emergence of America as a Great Power* [1961], though adhering to the outmoded view of McKinley as being propelled into war by public hysteria, is highly informative in interpreting the meaning of the last few weeks of negotiations between Washington and Madrid and in emphasizing the reasons for Spain's inability to compromise further in April 1898. A more recent work, Philip S. Foner's *The Spanish-Cuban-American War and the Birth of American Imperialism, 1895–1902*, 2 vols. [1972], adds a great deal of information about the Cuban rebellion but argues unconvincingly that the Cuban rebels could have won without American help, which they did not want, and that the United States intervened to protect the interests of monopoly capitalism from the creation of a radical independent Cuban government.)

The familiar story of the war itself belongs in military and naval histories. Spanish forces were no match for even the ill-prepared Americans, and by the time an armistice was signed on August 12, 1898, the United States had already captured Cuba and Puerto Rico, and, in the war's most dramatic event (if we can take the liberty of setting aside Teddy Roosevelt's claims for San Juan Hill) Commodore George Dewey had defeated the Spanish fleet at Manila on May 1, 1898, ushering in a long train of important consequences.

During the war Spain received much sympathy from the nations of continental Europe, but nothing more. The French envoy to Washington, who on July 8, 1898, described Americans as "ignorant, brutal, and quite capable of carelessly destroying the complicated European structure," arranged the armistice a month later. Great Britain was friendlier. She not only welcomed America into the ranks of the great imperial powers, but expelled one of Spain's agents from Canada on questionable evidence while winking at American espionage activities based in Gibraltar, denied coal to a Spanish fleet off Egypt, helped Americans get in touch with the exiled Filipino leader Emilio Aguinaldo, delayed the official proclamation of her lease of Mirs Bay from China so that American ships would not have to be ordered out, and allowed Dewey's headquarters in the Philippines to send messages to Washington on the Hong Kong cable, thus fully justifying Spain's complaints of unneutral conduct. (The details are in R. G. Neale, *Great Britain and United States Expansion: 1898–1900* [1966] and described again, along with interesting general comments on the new Anglo-American understanding, in Bradford Perkins, *The Great Rapprochement: England and the United States, 1895–1914* [1968].)

The British also responded favorably to the American annexation of Hawaii, finally accomplished in 1898. This affair had been in limbo since Cleveland's repudiation of the 1893 treaty, and anti-imperialists hoped that McKinley, too, would turn a deaf ear to the annexationists. Instead, he sent a new treaty to the Senate in June 1897. Supporters were unable to get the necessary two-thirds majority and the project stalled, but when war with Spain intervened the administration had renewed reason to push for annexation and sidestepped the problem of getting a two-thirds majority in the Senate by requesting action through a joint resolution, which required simple majority approval of both houses of Congress. All the old expansionist arguments reappeared in the debate on Hawaii: duty and glory, economic advantage, security for the west coast of the mainland, and the prevention of foreign incursions in a U.S. sphere of influence (a lively issue after 1897 when Japan clashed with Hawaii over its banning of Japanese immigration and protested in Washington against the new annexation treaty). Dewey's *coup de main* at Manila encouraged annexationist sentiment and added to the list of motives. The United States was now deeply implicated in East Asian affairs, which meant that Hawaii, long coveted as a mid-Pacific bastion for the defense of the west coast and future isthmian canal, now seemed an indispensable stepping-stone to Asia. "To maintain our flag in the Philippines," declared the New York *Sun*, "we must raise our flag in Hawaii." After long debates, the House approved the annexation resolution 290–91 in June and the Senate 42–21 in July. The nuptials between the United States and Hawaii were finally concluded only when the lovely islands had come to be desired not so much for themselves as for their invaluable help in sustaining the new American thrust toward East Asia, and when the impact of the New Paradigm made action essential that had shortly before seemed merely optional. (Various aspects of this episode are emphasized in several general works, such as LaFeber's *The New Empire*, Young's *Rhetoric of Empire*, and May's *Imperial Democracy*. Invaluable works concentrating specifically on Hawaii include William A. Russ, Jr., *The Hawaiian Republic (1894–98) and Its Struggle To Win Annexation* [1961]; S. K. Stevens, *American Expansion in Hawaii, 1842–1898* [1945]; and the following works by Merze Tate: *The United States & the Hawaiian Kingdom, A Political History* [1965], *Hawaii: Reciprocity or Annexation* [1968], and "Great Britain and the Sovereignty of Hawaii," *Pacific Historical Review*, XXXI, November 1962. All substantiate the impetus given to Hawaiian annexation by the emergence of the United States as a Far Eastern power.)

The sudden flush of victory in war produced a flurry of other imperialist proposals. Congress again resounded with the rhetoric of Davy Crockett spread-eaglism: America would expand from the frozen wastes of the Yukon to the frigid reaches of Cape Horn, gobbling up every island in the Caribbean. She would plunge into the contest for China. Interest in the Virgin Islands reappeared, especially when a rumor circulated in 1900 of Germany's interest in them (Germany was indeed tempted, but not enough to risk offending the United States). The thought of carrying the world's primitives into the modern age by means of Anglo-Saxon government, the little red schoolhouse, sanitary reform, and Yankee work habits inspired many Americans, including those on the Insular Commission who predicted that with American schools "in every valley and upon every hilltop in Porto Rico . . . the cloud of ignorance will disappear as the fog flies before the morning sun." More prosaically, the U.S. Naval Board advocated retention of the Philippines and acquisition of island bases in the Marianas, off the Chinese coast and the western coast of South America, and in the Caribbean.

The McKinley administration had more modest and precise goals in mind. Some it achieved without arrangements with other powers, such as the annexation of Hawaii in 1898 and occupation of Wake Island, between Hawaii and Guam, early in 1899, but other objectives required negotiations with Spain in Paris, where peace talks began October 1, 1898. McKinley chose his representatives with considerable cunning: former Secretary of State William R. Day, full of doubts about annexing the Philippines but a McKinley man, much respected by his colleagues; Whitelaw Reid of the New York *Tribune*, a Republican luminary and unabashed imperialist; and three senators who would have to vote on (and presumably defend) their own handiwork: William P. Frye and Cushman K. Davis, both Republican expansionists, and George Gray, a Democratic anti-imperialist. When McKinley sent them off to France he had not yet disclosed his decision on the Philippines. Soon after Reid's arrival in Paris, Spain's ambassador to France entreated him: "do not forget that we are poor; do not forget that we are vanquished; do not forget that after all it was Spain that discovered America; do not forget that this is the first great war you have had with a nation on the continent of Europe, or with any foreign nation; that you have had an astonishing victory, and that you cannot complete it without showing magnanimity" (from the fascinating H. Wayne Morgan, ed., *Making Peace with Spain: The Diary of Whitelaw Reid, September–December, 1898* [1965]). But as negotiations proceeded, it was Spain that urged the United States to annex Cuba, apparently in an attempt to shift to the Americans Cuba's $400 million debt, most of it incurred in the war against the rebels. McKinley's delegates would have none of it. The United States had solemnly forsworn annexing Cuba and would soon enough get what it wanted through a protectorate and control of Guantanamo Bay. The United States demanded cession of Puerto Rico, however, and—to satisfy the navy—the island of Guam in the Marianas. The most important issue at the conference was the fate of the Philippines, more than seven thousand islands with a population of about seven million people. After a brief hesitation, the administration demanded these, too, and received them in exchange for a face-saving payment of $20 million to Spain. The completed treaty was signed on December 10, 1898.

Most historians until recently have described the annexation of the Philippines as an accidental quirk, ordered reluctantly by a president who scarcely knew where they were. Annexation *was* "accidental" in that it would never have occurred had war with Spain been avoided, but the Philippines did not drop out of the blue into the lap of a dumbfounded McKinley. Influential Americans knew of the Philippines, and of Aguinaldo's insurrection against Spain, if only through articles on these subjects that appeared in important domestic periodicals in 1896 and 1897. Naval officers had formed contingency plans for attacking the Philippines in 1895 and 1896 (John A. S. Grenville, "American Naval Preparations for War with Spain, 1896–1898," *Journal of American Studies*, II, April 1968; and Grenville and Young, *Politics, Strategy and American Diplomacy*), and McKinley, who knew of these plans as early as September 1897, neither objected to them nor hesitated to approve orders for Dewey to prepare their execution a few weeks before the war began. During the war itself, the president took several deliberate steps that pointed toward annexation. A perfect opportunity for disentanglement appeared immediately after Dewey's victory; McKinley could have treated it as a mere tactical triumph and sent the commodore off to other points. Instead, before knowing for certain the full extent of the victory and without consulting Congress, McKinley called for volunteers to serve in the Philippines and immediately dispatched troops to occupy Manila. The first contingent of 11,000, almost double Dewey's request, began arriving by the end of June and more soon followed. On August 13, one day after the armistice, the troops seized Manila from the Spanish garrison and refused, in accordance with explicit orders, to allow Filipino insurrectionists to participate in the action. In Washington, such "large policy" imperialists as Mahan and Lodge were content for the moment to annex only Manila Harbor, leaving the rest to Spain. Soon, however, McKinley and his advisers decided that Manila would be militarily indefensible without the rest of Luzon; shortly thereafter, they determined that Luzon's defense would require possession of the rest of the Philippines. Even Aguinaldo remarked that total annexation was preferable to a partial one which would lead to "partition and a subsequent history similar to Poland's." As a result of this snowballing process of reasoning, the U.S. delegation in Paris eventually received orders to demand *all* the Philippines; annexing Luzon alone could "not be justified on political, commercial, or humanitarian grounds."

Exactly when McKinley decided on this course has been much debated. Ernest R. May contends that it was only after a two-week Midwestern speaking tour convinced him in early October that the public wanted the Philippines. A more plausible explanation, however, is that the methodical and taciturn Ohioan had determined to annex all the Philippines as early as June and was merely waiting for the people to catch up before making his decision public. He was not trying to outflank public opinion, and it was not for lack of alternatives that he favored annexation, although it must be conceded that, once troops were ordered to occupy Manila, it would have been hard for any president—even an anti-imperialist one—to reverse the trend toward annexation. Almost no one in the United States favored returning the islands to Spain. A protectorate was unsuitable as an option because it would burden the United States with heavy responsibilities but give it inadequate authority for sustaining them. Only a few anti-imperialists supported immediate independence for the Filipino "republic" proclaimed by Aguinaldo in June 1898 since most Americans believed that its result would be internal chaos, foreign intervention, and partition. The potential diplomatic complications of immediate independence were formidable. No country made a concerted effort to keep the Philippines out of U.S. hands, but at least four powers threatened to collide headlong in the wake of a decision to turn them loose. British leaders urged Americans to bite the bullet and take the Philippines but made it clear that Britain would want them otherwise. Japan applauded the idea of U.S. possession, partly to gain America's blessing for her activities in Korea, but especially to demonstrate her opposition to having the islands fall under the control of any other power. Similarly, Russia saw nothing in American policy to worry about but was fearful that Britain might somehow benefit from the situation. The driest tinder in the Philippines box was Germany; the commanders of her large naval contingent observing the goings-on in Manila were openly discourteous to Dewey though under strict orders to cause no trouble. The friction in Manila Harbor was symbolic of the fact that Berlin, more than any other capital, was prepared to make a powerful grab for the Philippines if the Americans backed off (James K. Eyre, Jr., "Japan and the American Annexation of the Philippines," *Pacific Historical Review*, XI, March 1942, and "Russia and the American Acquisition of the Philippines," *Mississippi Valley Historical Review*, XXVIII, March 1942; Thomas A. Bailey, "Dewey and the Germans at Manila Bay," *American Historical Review*, XLV, October 1939).

All the above factors would have been serious stumbling blocks for a president who wanted to get rid of the Philippines, but McKinley did not. First of all, moral and ideological impulses were working their effect on him, as is evident from the conclusion to his famous account of how he made his decision on the Philippines; "I am not ashamed to tell you, gentlemen," he confessed to a visiting delegation of fellow Methodists, "that I went down on my knees and prayed Almighty God for light and guidance more than one night," then explained that late one night the reasons in favor of annexation came to him, the last of which was "That there was nothing left for us to do but to take them all, and to educate the Filipinos, and uplift and civilize and Christianize them and by God's grace do the very best we could by them, as our fellow men, for whom Christ also died." But McKinley had a far more practical reason, too. He wanted to strengthen America's political and commercial foothold in East Asia, and from the Philippines the United States would be better able to defend its commercial interests in China and improve its political maneuverability in the region. In the words of an officer of the American Asiatic Association, an influential business lobby: "Had we no interests in China, the possession of the Philippines would be meaningless." As Professor Braisted notes in his *The United States Navy in the Pacific*, the U.S. Naval Board looked upon a base in the Philippines as a key outpost that would be of incalculable value in protecting American trade with China against European incursions. One official wrapped the whole argument up when he described the Philippines as America's "pickets of the Pacific, standing guard at the entrances to trade with the millions of China and Korea, French Indo-China, the Malay Peninsula, and the islands of Indonesia." Precisely because McKinley's decisions seemed so far-reaching in their implications, they aroused vigorous opposition from anti-imperialists. The opponents of American imperialism included members of both political parties, leading political independents, businessmen, writers and intellectuals, and a few labor leaders and progressive reformers—people like Grover Cleveland, William Jennings Bryan, Thomas B. Reed, Benjamin Harrison, Carl Schurz, E. L. Godkin, Andrew Carnegie, Mark Twain, William Dean Howells, William James, Samuel Gompers, and Jane Addams. The most energetic and vocal among them were political independents, most of them elderly, from New England. Although the Spanish-American War had caused much headshaking among them, the annexations that followed, especially that of the Philippines, really galvanized their opposition.

Historians of the "economic" school have tended to discount the anti-imperialists as genuine dissenters. W. A. Williams characterizes them as "men who understood and advocated the very kind of informal empire created by the inherent imbalance of the marketplace relationship between the advanced industrial Metropolis and the poor, backward, agrarian societies" (*The Great Evasion* [1964]). They opposed formal imperialism because the informal variety was adequate to American socioeconomic needs, less expensive, and less messy. This appraisal, at the very best, is exceedingly one-sided. As this author in *Twelve Against Empire: The Anti-Imperialists, 1898-1900* (1968) and E. Berkeley Tompkins in *Anti-Imperialism in the United States: The Great Debate, 1890-1920* (1970) demonstrate, few anti-imperialists were especially concerned about economic issues. The core of their opposition was their belief that imperialism was a total contradiction of American moral and political traditions. They feared that the practice of imperialism abroad would erode freedom at home and held that it was immoral for the United States to deny independence to the Philippines for the sake of its own ambitions. Anti-imperialists saw great danger in extending American diplomatic interests to the Far East and equal peril in trying to incorporate "alien races" into the U.S. political system. Many anti-imperialists were far more than just critical of imperialism; they were desolated by their conviction that this imperial adventure marked the abandonment of the national mission and provided indisputable proof that America could no longer be considered superior in morality and wisdom to other nations. (Daniel B. Schirmer's *Republic or Empire: American Resistance to the Philippine War* [1972], while taking quite a different tack from Williams, also emphasizes economic and class issues. Differences and similarities between his book and those by Beisner and Tompkins are described in the Bibliographical Essay, p. 149.

Anti-imperialists were particularly appalled by the horrors of the Filipino insurrection, which began in February 1899 two months after McKinley claimed U.S. sovereignty over the Philippines and defined American policy there as one of "benevolent assimilation." It took three years to put down the last vestiges of rebellion—and by that time the torture of captives, burning of native villages, use of a Spanish-style reconcentration policy, and the deaths of perhaps a half million Filipinos had badly soured the taste of America's imperial apple (Leon Wolff, *Little Brown Brother* [1961]). But, ironically, the first reports of the uprising, coming just as the Senate was on the verge of voting, probably helped to save the Paris peace treaty, narrowly approved 57–27 on February 9, 1899; a switch of two votes would have meant its defeat. Also contributing to its passage was William Jennings Bryan's decision to support it in order—as he thought—to eliminate Spain from the picture and free the United States to grant independence to the Philippines, which in turn would free him to concentrate on domestic issues in the 1900 election campaign. As Paolo E. Coletta has shown ("Bryan, McKinley and the Treaty of Paris, *Pacific Historical Review*, XXVI, May 1957), Bryan's strategy probably influenced few if any senators to vote in favor of ratification. On the other hand, at least two of the nineteen Democrats and silverite allies who supported the treaty would almost certainly have voted negatively (and thus defeated the pact) had Bryan come out foursquare against it and made it a party issue. On the Republican side, only two New Englanders impervious to the

New Paradigm voted against the treaty, but many more with misgivings about territorial annexations were reluctantly held in line by effective administration lobbying. How fragile the support for administration policy was became apparent eight days after ratification when only 29 votes could be mustered to oppose a resolution calling for American control over the Philippines to end as soon as the Filipinos established "a stable and independent government. . . ." The votes in favor also numbered only 29, however, and Vice-President Garret Hobart's opposing vote defeated the resolution.

Some Americans, including certain anti-imperialists, maintained that McKinley had allowed the United States to be lured into the Far East in order to serve British interests. This criticism underestimated the government's newly developed capacity to adopt policies for its own good reasons, and one of these policies, carried out in the teeth of constant vocal oppositon, was the forging of closer ties with Great Britain. Her friendliness during the war with Spain, her rebuff of a German proposal that the United States relinquish its position in either Hawaii or Samoa (Joseph W. Ellison, "The Partition of Samoa: A Study in Imperialism and Diplomacy," *Pacific Historical Review*, VIII, September 1939), and her support of the decision to annex the Philippines all seemed to justify the hands-across-the-sea enthusiasm that swept up many Americans. Leaders of both governments took pains to cultivate the mood. Britain's Colonial Secretary Joseph Chamberlain wrote John Hay in 1898: "I should rejoice in an occasion in which we could fight side by side. The good effect of it would last for generations." And Hay, by then secretary of state, remarked a year later: "As long as I stay here, no action shall be taken contrary to my conviction that the indispensable feature of our foreign policy should be a friendly understanding with England."

Concrete results of this rapprochement were few but important. Congress quashed legislation hostile to British shipping interests, British diplomats and naval officers cooperated with the Americans in the suppression of the Philippine rebellion, and the U.S. government conducted a slightly pro-British neutrality policy during the Boer War despite overwhelmingly pro-Boer feelings on the part of the American public. In 1901 Britain's first lord of the admiralty decided that the Americans had become so friendly that in the future all British naval construction planning should be based on the assumption that the United States fleet was a permanently nonhostile force, without even hypothetical exceptions. But the most substantial result of rapprochement was the long-awaited settlement of the canal question in the Hay-Pauncefote Treaty of 1901, which abrogated the vexatious Clayton-Bulwer Treaty of 1850 and gave the United States the go-ahead to build, arm, and control a canal of its own. The Senate had so mutilated a 1900 version of the treaty with amendments that the British rejected it as humiliating, yet the agreement they came around to accepting a year later was, in effect, the very one the Senate had insisted upon. In this instance, Hay and McKinley displayed a less realistic awareness of America's diplomatic needs than did those who demanded a revision of the 1900 accord that would delete a provision neutralizing the canal in wartime, and eliminate another that would have provided for other powers to join in guaranteeing the canal's neutrality. Theodore Roosevelt in particular opposed this last provision on the grounds that it would lead to European meddling in the Western Hemisphere.

The senators and T.R. got their way, but only because Britain was so concerned about the Boer War and her isolated position in Europe. In fact, though the Anglo-American rapprochement stemmed partly from a mutual awareness of similar interests in Asia and the Caribbean and a shared interest in imperialism, its most important source was the decline of Britain's strength in Europe and of its power vis-à-vis the United States. It must be remembered that it was Britain that gave in during the Venezuela crisis, conceded American supremacy in Hawaii and the Caribbean, surrendered its isthmian canal rights, and in 1903 yielded once more, this time to the U.S. position on the Alaska-Canadian boundary dispute. John Hay was aware of this, writing in 1900: "All I have ever done with England is to have wrung great concessions out of her with no compensation."

And this is exactly how his countrymen wanted it. Indeed, partly because of the continuing suspicions of anti-imperialists, German and Irish immigrants, isolationists, and other unreconstructed Anglophobes, the new transatlantic friendship was somewhat tenuous at best, marked by a certain "forced, hothouse quality resulting from wartime emotionalism [that] could not long outlive the [Spanish-American] war" (C. S. Campbell, Jr., "Anglo-American Relations, 1897–1901," in Paolo E. Coletta, ed., *Threshold to American Internationalism: Essays on the Foreign Policies of William McKinley* [1970]). In fact, one historian describes the eighties and nineties as an era of increasing American rage against Great Britain (Edward P. Crapol, *America for Americans: Economic Nationalism and Anglophobia in the Late Nineteenth Century* [1973]). Certainly many disagreements between the two countries still lay in the future.

THE OPEN DOOR POLICY

The Open Door notes of 1899–1900—the last major episode in nineteenth-century American diplomacy—were once mistakenly interpreted as a British invention and one of the fruits of the rapprochement (A. Whitney Griswold, *The Far Eastern Policy of the United States* [1938]). In reality, the Open Door policy was a direct outgrowth of traditional American views on the Far East, established as official policy in 1899–1900 to defend U.S. interests threatened by the "carving-up" of China. At stake for America was her new reputation as a world power, which would suffer if she stood by idly while China was partitioned, and specific business interests now generally considered to be vitally important to the American economy. The fate of various capital-investment projects, which were few in number and considered by the government to be more trouble than they were worth, did not concern Washington officials nearly as much as the growing Chinese market for U.S. exports, especially cotton textiles, illuminating oil, flour, lumber, and iron and steel products. The amounts of money involved were unimpressive compared to either British exports to China, which accounted for two-thirds of all Chinese purchases from abroad, or American exports to other countries. But American exports to China did rank second to Britain's and had doubled in value from 1896 to 1899. By 1900 the China market seemed crucial to the cotton textiles industry, following a decade during which exports to China had risen from slightly over $7 million to nearly $24 million, almost 50 percent of the industry's foreign sales. Moreover, Americans who calculated the importance of U.S. interests in China were not looking at current levels of trade but those of the future, which they thought of in grandiose terms ("a shirt on every Chinaman's back").

Beginning in the fall of 1897, the imperialist scavengers began feeding on the Chinese carcass. In a six-month period starting with the German seizure of Kiaochow in November 1897, five nations extorted leaseholds and spheres of influence from the beleaguered Chinese: Germany and Russia in Manchuria, North China, and the Shantung Peninsula; Great Britain in Shantung, Kowloon (opposite Hong Kong) and the Yangtze Valley; Japan (ejected from Manchuria in 1895 by Germany, Russia, and France) in Fukien province across the straits from her new possession of Formosa; and France in the south near her holdings in Indochina. What American officials would do—nervous about the economy, newly inclined to espy vital U.S. interests in Asia and translate their views into action—was not at first clear. The appropriate questions, however, were not hard to formulate, especially concerning northern China and Manchuria where two-thirds of American exports to China were sold and where Germany and especially Russia had now firmly lodged themselves. What if the ports were closed to American goods, or discriminatory harbor duties were placed on the vessels carrying them? What if unequal tariffs were imposed on U.S. products? What if higher railway freight rates were charged for carrying American goods from seaports to the interior than for transporting those of the country controlling the area?

At first, the administration seemed sanguine. Secretary of

State John Sherman even suggested that the optimum condition for American profits might be a China segmented and organized by foreign powers. Metropolitan chambers of commerce and newspapers, however, soon raised a clamor for strong U.S. action, and a group of businessmen organized as the Committee on American Interests in China (later the American Asiatic Association) carried out a thorough lobbying campaign (C. S. Campbell, Jr., *Special Interests and the Open Door Policy* [1951]). As Thomas J. McCormick points out, none of this pressure was really necessary since, Sherman's complacency notwithstanding, the McKinley administration had repeatedly demonstrated great concern with China during its first year in office; it negotiated for an expansion of the areas in China where American businessmen could reside, encouraged missionaries to gather information on Chinese commercial conditions, urged China to participate in American trade expositions, and made a vain attempt to remove imposts leveled by the Chinese on goods moving from one province to another. But the administration had no interest in acquiring a sphere of influence of its own. This would have set the anti-imperialist hornets buzzing again and put unwelcome burdens on a government with its hands already full of new overseas possessions and problems. Besides, since the areas where American businessmen were having their greatest success were already fenced off by Russia and Germany, staking out a plot for themselves on untried soil looked less than promising. Finally, as McCormick has written, "a small slice of the pie (which is all partitioning could offer) held little attraction for men who wanted (and thought they could get) the major share of the [entire Chinese] market."

In March 1898 Great Britain suggested to the United States that they take united action to preserve the open door, but Washington politely rejected the overture. The Cuban affair, about to culminate in war, required all the administration's attention; in any case, it preferred unilateral action to a cooperative initiative. By the summer of 1899, however, things had changed enough to make American action now seem both desirable and feasible. The war with Spain was over and the peace treaty ratified. Ownership of the Philippines bolstered confidence in America's ability to move boldly and stimulated public interest in China, as did a spate of journalistic pieces on Chinese affairs. Pressure from businessmen mounted. Finally, the international kaleidoscope stopped its motion at a propitious point when Britain, Japan, and Germany all indicated almost simultaneously that they might welcome some sort of open-door understanding in China. This left Russia, bristling menacingly in Manchuria.

The problem for John Hay was to find some way of getting Russia into line without risking a rebuff that would permanently discredit the open-door principle and damage American prestige. Russia gave him an opening in August 1899 with a policy statement that seemed to endorse the principle of equal commercial opportunity within its zone. Hay grabbed his chance, even though the Russian ukase had made no reference to railroad rates, and on September 6 dispatched the first Open Door notes, drafted by his astute adviser on the Far East, William W. Rockhill. He sent his first group of notes to Germany, Russia, and Great Britain, and later sent copies to Japan, France, and Italy. In them he asked each of the powers with a sphere of influence or leasehold to agree to the following four points and help persuade others to agree as well: (1) keep all "treaty" ports open; (2) maintain China's own tariff rates indiscriminately on all goods, including those of the locally residing imperial power; (3) impose no discriminatory harbor dues on ships of other nationalities; and (4) maintain nondiscriminatory railroad charges in the interior of the sphere or leasehold. A phrase calling on China to collect its own customs revenue has led some to suggest that Hay was making an oblique effort to undermine the whole spheres-of-influence system (Paul A. Varg, "William Woodville Rockhill and the Open Door Notes," *Journal of Modern History*, XXIV, December 1952), but this is unlikely in light of the fact that he neither consulted nor addressed a note to China herself until she made pointed inquiries. Far from challenging the system, Hay was trying to protect American interests within it and phrased his notes to apply only to the areas controlled by foreign powers rather than to China generally. It should also be added that he said nothing about equal rights in building railroads, establishing mines, or making other capital investments. Although he had defined his goals with caution, Hay could take credit for a low-cost triumph for American commercial diplomacy and the political fortunes of McKinley and the Republican Party if his demands won acceptance. There was, of course, one flaw in his policy that might render it totally futile: neither he nor anyone else in the administration was prepared to back up U.S. demands with force, or even the threat of force. The New Paradigm of 1899 did not encompass that level of risk-taking in Asia.

All would depend on the reception to Hay's notes. As this story has usually been told, none of the powers accepted Hay's terms, but he publicly announced that they *had* done so in a move that some commentators have described as a brilliant diplomatic stroke that caught the great powers off balance and forced them into line, but others have characterized as ineffectual and dangerously misleading to the American people. By contrast, some recent accounts, like McCormick's *China Market*, persuasively establish that Hay managed the entire affair with impressive subtlety but to mixed results. Working on the easiest marks first and reserving the Russians for last, he supervised separate negotiations with each power, hoping to avoid a flat rejection from one that would negate earlier acceptances from others and so build an atmosphere of unanimous agreement ("If everyone else goes along, I will, too"). Britain accepted his terms generally but without reference to Hong Kong or Kowloon and made her acceptance conditional on agreement by the other powers; Japan, Italy, and France all accepted quickly but conditionally; and Germany added its conditional assent only after strenuous discussions. The Russians now found themselves in a box. Their position in Manchuria was not totally secure, and they did not want to incur the suspicion of everyone by undoing all the conditional acceptances with a flat rejection of Hay's note. They stalled and argued tenaciously but finally "accepted" early in 1900.

The Russian response was elaborately hedged and made no allusion to the question of railroad rates. What to do? Hay first tried to press the Russians, but they relented only to the point of permitting him to describe their reply as "favorable." Thus on March 20, 1900, despite the absence of a single unconditionaly positive reply, Hay announced that the United States had received "favorable" responses from all parties. Certainly this was a bluff of sorts, but it was not the crude trick of which he has been accused. Nor, contrary to once-accepted interpretations, did he delude himself into thinking that his actions had "saved" China (Raymond G. Esthus, "The Changing Concept of the Open Door, 1899–1910," *Mississippi Valley Historical Review*, XLVI, December 1959, and *Theodore Roosevelt and the International Rivalries* [1970]), or suppose that the United States would or could intervene if one of the other countries chose to upset the delicate Asian balance of power with a grab for control in China. He knew that both America's limited interests and unenthusiastic public opinion would rule out such intervention.

The difficulty in making a low-risk policy pay off became clear later in 1900 during the Boxer Rebellion, which threatened to trigger a new wave of partitioning. The rebellion, led by youths but connived at by Chinese officials and the Dowager Empress herself, resulted in widespread looting and the murder of many foreigners, especially Christian missionaries, and their Chinese converts. The Boxers killed several "barbarians" in Peking's foreign quarter, including the German minister, and then laid siege to it. U.S. Minister Edwin Conger begged Washington to cooperate fully with the other powers in staging a rescue expedition, but the administration—busy dodging the slings and arrows of anti-imperialists at home and tracking down Aguinaldo's rebels in the Philippines—was not eager to send troops to China, abandon its independent stance on Chinese affairs, or contribute to foreign occupation and a new round of partitioning, the exact opposite of what McKinley and

Hay wanted. In the end, however, the United States did take part because its leaders saw more danger to both prestige and commerce in standing aside while others dominated the expedition. Five thousand troops were eventually sent from the Philippines (perhaps the only case when control of those islands actually buttressed U.S. China policy as predicted in the rhetoric of 1898–99) to join a combined force of 19,000 troops that finally relieved the siege in mid-August 1900.

On July 3, 1900, Hay sent out his second Open Door note, this one a circular requiring no answer. On the face of it, this note seemed a significant enlargement of the U.S. commitment in China, both in its reference to safeguarding the open-door principle in "all parts of the Chinese Empire" and its statement that it was American policy to "preserve Chinese territorial and administrative entity. . . ." Hay was no fool, however, an elementary fact that many historians have refused to acknowledge. He was painfully aware how unprepared his country was to back up his diplomatic language. What he was probably trying to do in 1900 was encourage moderate conduct on the part of the Boxer expedition allies with a conspicuous declaration that the United States would not exploit the crisis by doing anything to weaken the Chinese state or obstruct equal commercial treatment for all parties in China and hoped the others would follow suit. The note rested on the hope that none of the other powers would risk disrupting the delicate balance of power in either Asia or Europe by a sudden grab for exclusive control in China. According to some historians the administration's hopes were even more modest than this. Paul A. Varg points out that in a memorandum from Assistant Secretary of State J. B. Moore to Hay only two days before the 1900 circular, Moore described the "idea of supporting the independence and integrity of China" as something that would conform to "the sentiments of our people" and defined America's "immediate interest" in Asia as the security of the Philippines (*The Making of a Myth: The United States and China, 1897–1912* [1968]). Akira Iriye claims that the purpose of Hay's second note was to squelch the U.S. Navy's intrigues for a Chinese base of its own

(*Across the Pacific: An Inner History of American–East Asian Relations* [1967]). Oddly enough, in November 1900, four months after he sent the circular, Hay suddenly made a move to acquire Samsa Bay, opposite Formosa, and then quickly withdrew the request when Japan raised objections. This episode is more significant than it seems at first glance since it demonstrates that the Open Door policy did not challenge foreign spheres of influence in China or preclude the possibility of America's acquiring one, provides evidence that the U.S. Navy wanted such a base (it continued to clamor for one until 1905), and supports Iriye's contention that Hay, as indicated by his quick withdrawal of the Samsa Bay request, was indeed engaged in a holding operation against the navy for control of China policy and that his operation was successful. (Michael H. Hunt, in *Frontier Defense and the Open Door: Manchuria in Chinese–American Relations, 1895–1911* [1973], depicts Hay as being both less certain and more ambitious in his goals than described here.)

The protocol negotiations that followed the suppression of the rebellion demonstrated the weakness of the American position. Almost alone among the powers, the United States supported only moderate punishment for the Chinese, since the New Paradigm in no way demanded gratuitously severe treatment of a people who were viewed as prospective customers for the American economic surplus. The final protocol of September 1901, which reflected the majority mood, was harsh, calling for the punishment and in some cases execution of various guilty Chinese, the erection of monuments where foreigners had been murdered and other outrages had occurred, a guarantee of an unfettered line of communications for foreigners from Peking to the sea, and reparations amounting to a third of a billion dollars. Nothing was said about enforcing the open door, and when Japan asked during the negotiations how far the United States was prepared to go in support of the doctrine, Hay replied that his government was not contemplating the use of force, either unilaterally or in league with others.

This unwillingness to back the open door with force is one

reason most historians have attacked the policy, but it has also been criticized for committing the United States to unessential and indefensible goals and for its false assumption that all other powers shared America's desire for an open China. In addition, critics have repeatedly pointed out that it was the caution of great powers in avoiding a world war over China, not Hay's genius or his Open Door policy, which actually prevented the further dismemberment of China, in his time at least.

Some of these criticisms are unfair because they exaggerate what McKinley and Hay actually hoped to achieve. McCormick, for instance, correctly points out that the attempt to support the open door with a combination of rhetoric, timely overtures, and minimal commitment of force was not really so quixotic since it came at a time when there was a "de facto balance of power" in China formed by Russia and France on one side and Britain and Japan on the other. Under these circumstances, "there was a good chance the powers would acquiesce" if the United States, acting as a "third force," "dramatically insisted that the status quo . . . be universally accepted. . . ." The path of retreat was always open if the going got rough, as it did after 1900. Hay, though disappointed not to accomplish more, knew where he stood and, instead of digging in to defend an untenable position, eventually pulled back, prudently muzzling further talk of defending China's "integrity" as he retreated (it was the Taft administration that unhappily resurrected that unrealistic objective). It was well that Hay knew when to retreat because, in clumsier hands than his, the Open Door policy could have proved a disaster, based as it was on a set of fantasies; in this the critics are certainly right. Marilyn B. Young has written that "the notion of a special friendship between China and America, of the riches of the China market, of America's role as balancer of powers in Asia, were all accepted as descriptions of the situation and not, as they were in fact, the possibilities merely. The American public was given to believe that its most vital national interests were involved in China, yet the commercial and financial interests which might have given substance to this claim were absent." Why, in spite of all this, the Open Door became a major United States "policy" was one of the less fortunate consequences of the New Paradigm. China did not have to be "objectively" important to the United States to *seem* important in the eyes of its leaders. "Americans looked to China for justification of their new self-image," writes Robert McClellan; "therefore it mattered little if the policy of the United States in China was based on actual conditions. What did matter was that any policy had to be formulated in accord with the concept of America's new role in world affairs" (*The Heathen Chinee: A Study of American Attitudes toward China, 1890–1905* [1970]).

During McKinley's successful reelection campaign in 1900 Republicans busily denied charges that they were guilty of the un-American sin of "imperialism." The GOP platform declared that "no thought of National aggrandizement has tarnished the high purpose" of the United States; Senator Henry Cabot Lodge, too, rejected the accusation of "imperialism" but did admit adherence to a policy of "expansion," which he took to be a positive good; and McKinley's running mate Theodore Roosevelt flatly declared that "nothing even remotely resembling 'imperialism' or 'militarism' " had been involved in recent events, which he described as the most current phase "of that policy of expansion which has been part of the history of America from the day when she became a nation." These men may have been fooling themselves, but their denials were probably sincere, as were their disclaimers of having plans for further territorial aggrandizement. The outstanding hallmark of the McKinley administration was not a headlong rush toward territorial expansion but the inauguration of America's new career as a world power, paralleling the advent of what we have called the New Paradigm. McKinley's part in this inaugural ceremony was eliminated by an assassin, but Theodore Roosevelt carried on—"the first president," H. Wayne Morgan writes, "to have no rest from complicated foreign issues, just as his generation of Americans was the first to pursue more than 'crisis diplomacy.' Foreign affairs were here to stay."

Harbingers

In 1900 the United States was already face to face with many of the issues that would head the agenda for American foreign relations experts in the twentieth century. Although no one was yet worried about Soviet Communism or the impact of air power and atomic weapons on national strategy, and the United States had not yet been drawn into the deadly web of European diplomacy that would soon ensnare the world in "the Great War," many enduring patterns had already been established. American and Russian interests were colliding for the first time in Manchuria, challenging the myth of a "natural" friendship between the two nations. Relations with Germany had steadily worsened owing to friction over Samoa, the Philippines, and China. Anglo-American relations, on the other hand, had become almost predictably friendly, although an occasional misunderstanding still occurred. Relations with China wavered back and forth for years, ranging from lukewarm to cordial, but a steady trend toward greater antagonism with Japan was already visible. Three developments around the year 1900 had limited America's freedom of action in Asian policymaking. The first was the acquisition of the Philippines, which nailed the United States down to an unprecedented military commitment in the Far East. The second was the Open Door policy, which, as interpreted by some of Hay's successors, increasingly cast the United States in the role of defender of China. The third was the growing conviction that events in Asia had an extremely important bearing on United States interests, or, more precisely stated, that Americans expected to gain economic sustenance from Asia in exchange for offering it guidance into the new world of democracy, Christianity, and commerce.

All three pointed toward conflict with Japan.

Relations between the United States and Latin America also proceeded logically from the base set by 1900. For many decades Americans had paid considerable attention to the affairs of this region, but without the benefit of a systematic Latin American "policy"; instead they periodically and unpredictably grabbed at nearby territory or meddled in the affairs of a neighboring country. But those with vision could see that the events of the nineties were auguries of a growing trend toward U.S. domination of the area, and in particular of the Caribbean, spurred on by the need to protect the security of the isthmian canal that was finally constructed after the Panamanian revolution of 1903. In 1904, Roosevelt's Corollary to the Monroe Doctrine formalized the new American attitude, and a series of interventions in the next two decades proved Washington's seriousness in enforcing it. By the end of the Wilson administration, the United States had become not only the uncontested arbiter of Caribbean questions, but the region's semicolonial master as well.

This mastery was not accomplished through the acquisition of formal colonies, for the surge of American colonialism ended in 1900. The leaders of the McKinley administration had never defined colonial gains as essential objects of U.S. policy but had rather stressed a general expansion of American political and economic interests abroad and the use of great energy to protect these interests. To achieve this goal they gave unprecedented attention to the systematic formulation and execution of U.S. foreign policy and thereby inaugurated a new era in American diplomatic history.

It goes beyond the scope of this book to describe how the New Paradigm of the 1890s was succeeded in later years by other, similarly abrupt, revolutions in American diplomatic patterns, though in a work already mentioned Michael Roskin persuasively suggests that such breaks occurred after World War I and the Versailles Treaty, again after Munich and Pearl Harbor, and most recently in the late 1960s when the Vietnam War provoked a profound reaction against the global pretensions and fears that were the hallmark of American foreign policy in the years from Franklin Roosevelt to Lyndon Johnson.

Some of the changes of the 1890s remain a part of American foreign policy to our own day, for better or worse. Since 1900 the United States government has never conducted diplomacy in the amateurish manner that was par for the course in the years of the Old Paradigm (though professional competence, of course, cannot necessarily be equated with wisdom). No administration since 1900, including those of Harding, Coolidge, and Hoover, has been content to return to the "isolationist" assumptions of the 1870s. And no president in the twentieth century has ever ignored the Far East with the aplomb of a Chester Arthur, or even a Grover Cleveland. The Harrisons, Blaines, Olneys, McKinleys, and Hays could not anticipate the revolutionary diplomatic changes that would come in the next seventy-five years, but they did know they had led the United States into a new and dangerous world of power politics and international contention. The prospect seemed to excite more than disturb them.

Bibliographical Essay

Some works on this period deserve to be called "essential." One of these is Walter LaFeber's *The New Empire: An Interpretation of American Expansion, 1860–1898* (Ithaca, 1963). Although LaFeber's book exaggerates the role of economic factors, is at times simplistic in its psychology, and occasionally borders on the unreliable in its use of evidence, *The New Empire* is a work that anyone retracing this chronological span must consider. By contrast, Foster R. Dulles's pleasantly written survey of the same era, *Prelude to World Power: American Diplomatic History, 1860–1900* (New York, 1965), was obsolete the day it was published. Another essential work, in the sense that every student of American expansionism should eventually make his way through its elaborately sardonic and erudite arguments, is Albert K. Weinberg, *Manifest Destiny: A Study of Nationalist Expansionism in American History* (Baltimore, 1935).

There are several other books that have been particularly important to my own understanding and interpretation of the subject. Some of them were valuable for removing the label of "mediocre" from the period, especially H. Wayne Morgan's *From Hayes to McKinley: National Party Politics, 1877–1896* (Syracuse, 1969), several biographical works, the LaFeber volume mentioned above, and Milton Plesur's *America's Outward Thrust: Approaches to Foreign Affairs, 1865–1890* (Dekalb, Ill., 1971). The latter book, while unexciting in style and interpretation, is important because Plesur does so many things for the pre-1890 era that others have left undone: he devotes unusual attention to such routine diplomatic subjects as the protection of U.S. citizens abroad, to the actual conduct of American exporters, and to such nondiplomatic phases of "foreign relations" as transatlantic travel. Despite the inclusion of the years 1865–90 in the title, the reader should be alerted that Plesur's book deals almost exclusively with the 1880s.

My own interpretation, as presented in this book, arose in part from a long-standing interest in reconciling the more persuasive parts of works by such market-expansionism historians as LaFeber, William A. Williams, and Thomas J. McCormick with the noneconomic interpretations they rejected. Among the writings that were of special help to me in this task and in the larger one of making sense of late-nineteenth-century American foreign policy are the following, mentioned here in the order in which I became familiar with them. First is Richard Hofstadter's subtle and suggestive essay, "Cuba, the Philippines, and Manifest Destiny," in *The Paranoid Style in American Politics and Other Essays* (New York, 1965), originally published in 1952, which first persuaded me of the importance of the "crisis" of the 1890s in producing change in American foreign relations. Next are the foreign policy sections of Robert H. Wiebe's *The Search for Order, 1877–1920* (New York, 1967), a trenchant analysis of the piecemeal character of U.S. diplomacy before the age of "policy" (the arrival of which he places around 1900–1905, in contrast to my dating) that suggested a new way to think about the palpable shift in U.S. diplomatic behavior in the 1890s. But since Wiebe's analysis lacked a convincing account of the causes of the shift from "incidents" to "policy," it was especially helpful to me to become acquainted with paradigm theory through Michael Roskin's "Turning Inward: The Effects of the Vietnam War on U.S. Foreign Policy" (Ph.D. dissertation, The American University, 1972) and Thomas S. Kuhn's *The Structure of Scientific Revolutions* (2d ed., Chicago, 1970), works that suggested a general framework for a number of the points I was eager to make. (An article, discovered much later, that might have suggested a similar interpretative approach is Ernest R. May, "The Nature of Foreign Policy: The Calculated vs. the Axiomatic," *Daedalus*, XCI [Fall 1962].) Finally, two other works are important because of the interesting points made in them on the inseparability of economic, political, and ideological impulses: David Healy, *US Expansionism: The Imperialist Urge in the 1890s* (Madison, 1970) and James A. Field, Jr., *America and the Mediterranean World, 1776–1882* (Princeton, 1969). Though his book is excessively eclectic in point of view, Healy's examination of the expedient use of the rhetoric of expanding markets by men whose main interest lay in expanding U.S. power casts doubt on the significance of much of the rhetorical evidence offered by LaFeber, Williams, and McCormick. Field's volume, which is concerned with an area of the world with little diplomatic significance for the United States in the latter part of the nineteenth century, does include an elegant analysis of the ideology behind America's traditional interest in foreign trade (it also demonstrates how common it was in the era of the Old Paradigm for diplomatic and economic initiatives to originate in the field rather than in Washington).

In addition to the works discussed above that influenced the general framework of this book, there are others that were essential to its execution and should be considered required reading for anyone wanting to probe more deeply into the subject. J. A. S. Grenville and G. B. Young's *Politics, Strategy and American Diplomacy: Studies in Foreign Policy, 1873–1917* (New Haven, 1966) presents new views on many important subjects ranging from the origins of the modern U.S. navy and the Venezuela crisis to the causes of war in 1898 and the history of the plan to attack Manila. Grenville and Young are committed to no single view though they put little stock in economic interpretations and are inclined instead to emphasize the influence (usually pernicious) of domestic politics in foreign affairs. In *Imperial Democracy: The Emergence of America as a Great Power* (New York, 1961) Ernest R. May makes clear how great the gap was that separated Washington from Madrid at the time of McKinley's 1898 war message and, in a unique survey, analyzes the reactions of leading European countries to the dramatic assertion of America's international power from 1895 to 1900. Unfortunately, his book also harbors some strange contradictions: McKinley is depicted as having pursued a definite Cuban policy so radically opposed to Spain's goals as to make war all but inevitable, and yet May ignores his own evidence and falls back on traditional accounts to show that McKinley was pushed into war against his will by public opinion and, weather vane-like, ordered the annexation of the Philippines only because he believed that the state of opinion left no politic alternative.

Four historians have made especially valuable contributions on Far Eastern affairs. Marilyn B. Young's *Rhetoric of Empire: American China Policy, 1895–1901* (Cambridge, Mass., 1968) and "American Expansion 1870–1900: The Far East," in Barton J. Bernstein, ed., *Towards a New Past: Dissenting Essays in American History* (New York, 1967, 1968) are less well known than they should be, probably because of their uninformative titles and their author's modesty in generalizing from her evidence. Young is especially good at assessing the now-bold, now-cautious, American policy in China and estimating the relative importance of political and economic factors lying behind that policy. Less subtle but nevertheless important is Thomas J. McCormick's *China Market: America's Quest for*

Informal Empire, 1893–1901 (Chicago, 1967), a detailed and intriguing account of economic expansionism in China and its bearing on U.S. attitudes and decisions regarding the Philippines. This work suffers, however, from an underestimation of ideological and emotional influences, a deficiency for which Young's writings serve as a useful corrective. A brief version of some of McCormick's arguments appears in "Insular Imperialism and the Open Door: The China Market and the Spanish-American War," *Pacific Historical Review*, XXXII (May 1963). Another excellent book is William R. Braisted's *The United States Navy in the Pacific, 1897–1909* (Austin, 1958), based on material unfamiliar to most diplomatic historians, especially good on U.S. relations with the various powers in China, and revealing on much more than naval matters. Although now a half century old, Tyler Dennett's *Americans in Eastern Asia* (New York, 1922) remains indispensable to those interested in the details of U.S. Asian policy in the nineteenth century; the sort of work usually overlooked by teachers and students because of its age, this book richly deserves a paperback revival.

In order to gain a thorough understanding of the "markets" thesis, one should read William A. Williams's *The Tragedy of American Diplomacy* (2d rev. ed., New York, 1972) and *The Roots of the Modern American Empire: A Study of the Growth and Shaping of Social Consciousness in a Marketplace Society* (New York, 1969). Both books are profoundly serious efforts to discover the roots of what Williams sees as long-lived and tragic compulsions in American diplomacy. The main importance of the latter work lies in the author's lengthy analysis of his own intellectual progress and his massively-researched (and regrettably tedious) attempt to incorporate the agrarian sector into the economic interpretation of American foreign policy. All of Williams's books have passages of great power and insight. Unfortunately, they are also characterized by slipshod arguments, an attitude toward evidence that is sometimes downright manipulative, and a cavalier disregard for the many historians in the field who hold different views. Though not concerned with the period discussed in this book, a damaging exposé of

Williams's methods may be found in Robert James Maddox, "Another Look at the Legend of Isolationism in the 1920's," *Mid-America*, LIII (January 1971), incorporated in his later study, *The New Left and the Origins of the Cold War* (Princeton, 1973). For one of the best direct assaults on the substance of his (and LaFeber's) work on the late nineteenth century, see the essay by Paul S. Holbo, "Economics, Emotion, and Expansion: An Emerging Foreign policy," which appears in H. Wayne Morgan, ed., *The Gilded Age* (rev. and enlarged ed., Syracuse, 1970). Holbo's exposition of the complexity of such "economic" issues as tariff reform is especially valuable.

Many other books and articles, though perhaps not "essential" to the general reader, should also be mentioned here. Among the most valuable biographical studies are Glyndon G. Van Deusen, *William Henry Seward* (New York, 1967); Ernest N. Paolino, *The Foundations of the American Empire: William Henry Seward and U.S. Foreign Policy* (Ithaca, 1973); Allan Nevins, *Hamilton Fish: The Inner History of the Grant Administration*, 2 vols. (New York, 1936); William F. Livezey, *Mahan on Sea Power* (Norman, Okla., 1947); John A. Garraty, *Henry Cabot Lodge* (New York, 1953); Margaret Leech, *In the Days of McKinley* (New York, 1959); and H. Wayne Morgan, *William McKinley and His America* (Syracuse, 1963), though his brief synthesis, *America's Road to Empire: The War with Spain and Overseas Expansion* (New York, 1965), is actually a better book on diplomatic subjects.

Studies abound of U.S. relations with particular countries. On Britain see the invaluable if wordy H. C. Allen, *Great Britain and the United States* (New York, 1955); Bradford Perkins's helpful survey, *The Great Rapprochement: England and the United States, 1895–1914* (New York, 1968); Lionel M. Gelber's *The Rise of Anglo-American Friendship: A Study in World Politics, 1898–1906* (London, 1938), outmoded in some ways but on firm ground in emphasizing the limits of the rapprochement in the 1899–1901 period; R. G. Neale, *Great Britain and United States Expansion: 1898–1900* (East Lansing, 1966); C. S. Campbell, Jr., *Anglo-American Understanding, 1898–1903* (Baltimore,

1957); Alexander E. Campbell, *Great Britain and the United States, 1895–1903* (London, 1960); and, running against the tide of historiographical tradition, Edward P. Crapol, *America for Americans: Economic Nationalism and Anglophobia in the Late Nineteenth Century* (Westport, Conn., 1973), which stresses Anglo-American conflict rather than rapprochement. On France, see the useful if unexciting books by Henry Blumenthal, *A Reappraisal of Franco-American Relations, 1830–1871* (Chapel Hill, 1959) and *France and the United States: Their Diplomatic Relations, 1789–1914* (Chapel Hill, 1970). An excellent recent work on relations with Canada is Robert C. Brown, *Canada's National Policy, 1883–1900: A Study in Canadian-American Relations* (Princeton, 1964). In addition to the works by Young and McCormick on China, see Paul A. Varg, *The Making of a Myth: The United States and China, 1897–1912* (East Lansing, 1968) and Warren I. Cohen's excellent synthesis, *America's Response to China: An Interpretative History of Sino-American Relations* (New York, 1971). John K. Fairbank recommends that we look on America's China policy as a mere segment of a general "European" policy toward China in " 'American China Policy' to 1898: A Misconception," *Pacific Historical Review*, XXXIX (November 1970). Detailed studies of U.S. relations with particular Latin American nations, many of them published in the 1930s and 1940s—such as Ludwell L. Montague, *Haiti and the United States, 1714–1938* (Durham, 1940)—are still to be preferred to the capsule accounts and occasional distortions found in some of the available interpretive syntheses of American foreign policy.

Other works of importance on the Seward–Grant–Fish era include David Donald, *Charles Sumner and the Rights of Man* (New York, 1970), chock-full of "diplomatic" history, essential on Sumner's controversial role in foreign affairs, and rather harsh on Hamilton Fish; Tyler Dennett, "Seward's Far Eastern Diplomacy," *American Historical Review*, XXVIII (October 1922); Alfred J. and Kathryn A. Hanna, *Napoleon III and Mexico: American Triumph over Monarchy* (Chapel Hill, 1971), the best single book on this episode though not novel in interpretation; and Maureen M. Robson, "The *Alabama* Claims and the Anglo-American Reconciliation, 1865–71," *Canadian Historical Review*, XLII (March 1961), a fine short analysis of the circumstances that first delayed and then permitted a settlement of the *Alabama* claims.

On Blaine, see the indispensable articles by Russell H. Bastert, "Diplomatic Reversal: Frelinghuysen's Opposition to Blaine's Pan-American Policy in 1882," *Mississippi Valley Historical Review*, XLII (March 1956) and "A New Approach to the Origins of Blaine's Pan American Policy," *Hispanic American Historical Review*, XXXIX (August 1959). A different view of Blaine, more in the LaFeber-Williams tradition but more discriminating than either in its treatment of economic issues, is Tom E. Terrill, *The Tariff, Politics, and American Foreign Policy, 1874–1901* (Westport, Conn., 1973). An important study of the same period that helps restore it to respectful attention is David Pletcher's *The Awkward Years: American Foreign Relations under Garfield and Arthur* (Columbia, Mo., 1963). An impressive new work on the Samoan question, published several years after the author's untimely death, is R. P. Gilson, *Samoa 1830 to 1900: The Politics of a Multi-Cultural Community* (Melbourne, 1970).

The literature is especially rich on the late eighties and nineties, as might be expected. Richard Hofstadter's *Social Darwinism in American Thought, 1860–1915* (Philadelphia, 1945) is still useful, but the subject cries out for a richer analysis. Naval developments can be followed in Robert Seager II, "Ten Years before Mahan: The Unofficial Case for the New Navy, 1880–1890," *Mississippi Valley Historical Review*, XL (December 1953); Harold and Margaret Sprout, *The Rise of American Naval Power, 1776–1918* (Princeton, 1944); Kenneth J. Hagan, *American Gunboat Diplomacy and the Old Navy, 1877–1889* (Westport, Conn., 1973); and Walter R. Herrick, *The American Naval Revolution* (Baton Rouge, 1966), which also untangles the Haitian and Chilean affairs of 1889–92 and exposes Secretary of the Navy Tracy as the red-hot jingo in both. On Hawaiian developments, see Julius W. Pratt, *Expansionists of 1898: The Acquisition of Hawaii and the Spanish Islands* (Baltimore, 1936),

William A. Russ, Jr., *The Hawaiian Revolution (1893–94)* (Selins-grove, Pa., 1959), and Merze Tate, *The United States & the Hawaiian Kingdom, A Political History* (New Haven, 1965). The British perspective on the Venezuela crisis is available in John A. S. Grenville's *Lord Salisbury and Foreign Policy: The Close of the Nineteenth Century* (London, 1964).

Another significant book by Ernest R. May, though it is not free from serious conceptual and semantical problems (especially an unnecessarily narrow definition of "imperialism"), is *American Imperialism: A Speculative Essay* (New York, 1968), in which May makes an impressive effort to refine the concept of "public opinion," trace the influence of European attitudes on those of the United States, and determine through these means why the United States rejected "imperialism" in the 1870s, adopted it in 1898, and then abruptly dropped it for good shortly thereafter. An excellent summary on how McKinley got the United States firmly lodged in the Philippines many weeks before the Paris peace talks and why he eventually demanded annexation of the whole archipelago can be found in Paolo E. Coletta, "McKinley, the Peace Negotiations, and the Acquisi-tion of the Philippines," *Pacific Historical Review*, XXX (No-vember 1961). For an example of the kind of pulp-magazine history that should have been published in *Imaginary Tales*, see Timothy G. McDonald, "McKinley and the Coming of the War with Spain," *Midwest Quarterly*, VII (April 1966), who argues that a super-Machiavellian McKinley deliberately forced war on Spain in order to create an excuse for the seizure of the Philippines but delayed the start of hostilities until mid-April 1898 to give U.S. naval units time to get into position for their appointed task. Ingeniously argued but totally unconvincing and innocent of documentation.

Those interested in anti-imperialism might begin with Fred H. Harrington, "The Anti-Imperialist Movement in the United States, 1898–1900," *Mississippi Valley Historical Review*, XXII (September 1935), which stands up marvelously after forty years; then proceed to Christopher Lasch, "The Anti-Imperial-ists, the Philippines, and the Inequality of Man," *Journal of*

Southern History, XXIV (August 1958), which detects the racism of anti-imperialists but fails to recognize their more generous impulses; Robert L. Beisner, *Twelve Against Empire: The Anti-Imperialists, 1898–1900* (New York, 1968), which finds both the strengths and weaknesses of the anti-imperialist movement in its traditionalism and hostility to party politics, and "1898 and 1968: The Anti-Imperialists and the Doves," *Political Science Quarterly*, LXXXV (June 1970), which compares the movement with the contemporary American antiwar movement; Richard E. Welch, Jr., "Motives and Policy Objectives of Anti-Imperialists, 1898," *Mid-America*, LI (April 1969), a good summary that sees less racism in anti-imperialism than either Lasch or Beisner; E. Berkeley Tompkins, *Anti-Imperialism in the United States: The Great Debate, 1890–1920* (Philadelphia, 1970), a valuable survey of the facts which, however, portrays the anti-imperialists without their warts; and Daniel B. Schirmer, *Republic or Empire: American Resistance to the Philippine War* (Cambridge, Mass., 1972), a vigorous, present-minded, narrative of Boston anti-imperialism unfortunately saddled with the interesting but unconvincing thesis that anti-imperialism represented a struggle of the old mercantile elite (joined by labor, Negroes, and "youth") against imperialist bankers and manufacturers. Tompkins and Schirmer both exaggerate the progressive (or even radical) tendencies of the anti-imperialist movement, but they and Harrington, Beisner, and Welch all agree that the "anti's" were arguing about basic national goals, not tactics, in their campaign against the expansionists.

Still a good guide to the foreign policy significance of the 1900 election is Thomas A. Bailey, "Was the Presidential Election of 1900 a Mandate on Imperialism?" *Mississippi Valley Historical Review*, XXIV (June 1937). In addition to works already mentioned, Charles S. Campbell, Jr., *Special Business Interests and the Open Door Policy* (New Haven, 1951) and Raymond A. Esthus, "The Changing Concept of the Open Door, 1899–1910," *Mississippi Valley Historical Review*, XLVI (December 1959) are essential. Among the works badly needed is a careful scholarly inquiry into the Philippines Insurrection.

At present, we must rest content with Leon Wolff's journalistic indictment, *Little Brown Brother: How the United States Purchased and Pacified the Philippine Islands at the Century's Turn* (Garden City, N.Y., 1961) and Henry F. Graff's carefully compiled collection of sources, *American Imperialism and the Philippine Insurrection* (Boston, 1969).

Just as this book went to press, interesting essays on Seward, Fish, Blaine, and Mahan by, respectively, Gordon H. Warren, James B. Chapin, Lester D. Langley, and Kenneth J. Hagan, appeared in the first volume of Frank J. Merli and Theodore A. Wilson (eds.), *Makers of American Diplomacy* (New York, 1974).

INDEX